PUBLIC ATTITUDES TOWARD CHURCH AND STATE

AMERICAN POLITICAL INSTITUTIONS AND PUBLIC POLICY

Stephen J. Wayne
Series Editor

AMERICAN POLITICAL INSTITUTIONS AND PUBLIC POLICY

PUBLIC ATTITUDES TOWARD CHURCH AND STATE

TED G. JELEN
CLYDE WILCOX

M.E. Sharpe
Armonk, New York
London, England

Library of Congress Cataloging-in-Publication Data

Jelen, Ted G.
Public attitudes toward church and state / Ted G. Jelen and Clyde Wilcox.
p. cm. — (American political institutions and public policy)
Includes bibliographical references and index.
ISBN 1-56324-148-X (alk. paper). — ISBN 1-56324-149-8 (pbk. : alk. paper)
1. Church and state—United States—Public opinion.
2. Religion and state—United States—Public opinion.
3. United States—Public opinion.
I. Wilcox, Clyde, 1953–
II. Title. III. Series.
BR516.J45   1995
322′.1′0973—dc20   95-17896
CIP

Printed in the United States of America

The paper used in this publication meets the minimum requirements of
American National Standard for Information Sciences—
Permanence of Paper for Printed Library Materials,
ANSI Z 39.48-1984.

BM (c)   10   9   8   7   6   5   4   3   2   1
BM (p)   10   9   8   7   6   5   4   3   2   1

To William J. Wilcox

Contents

List of Tables

Foreword

The world bears witness to much sectarian religious violence. Bosnia, Northern Ireland, and, of course, the Middle East illustrate the extent and persistence of the problem. In the name of religion people fortify and fight for their beliefs. In the process they impinge on the interests, needs, and rights of others.

Americans, thankfully, have been spared much of this violence. Religious controversy in the United States has occurred primarily within the legal and political system rather than outside it.

Political conflict over religious beliefs is what we would expect in a free society that respects these beliefs but prohibits the antisocial behavior they may sometimes promote. The framers of the American Constitution got it right. Their solution to protecting the nation's rich but diverse religious heritage was to create a system in which religion and religious organizations could flourish but not dominate the social order. The constitutional embodiment of this solution was the First Amendment's establishment and free exercise clauses plus the absence in the document of any religious tests for holding office.

The politics of protecting the free exercise of religion and preventing the establishment of religion have changed over the years as succeeding generations have attempted to redefine constitutional boundaries in a manner that conforms to their beliefs and practices. Today those politics impact on the policy debates over the role of government in society, the parameters of federalism, the dimensions of the welfare state, and the issues of crime, punishment, and due process of law. How far should government go in permitting or preventing religious activities? Should the national government impose standards on the states in the name of basic individual rights? Where should the line be drawn between promoting the general welfare and indirectly aiding religion or between maintaining law and order and curtailing religious activities?

These questions raise difficult issues that public officials must address. In a democracy where legislators enact public policy, where executives implement that policy, and where judges adjudicate cases arising from that policy, government officials must be aware of public opinion and, to some extent, responsive to it. They must balance their responsiveness with their constitutional oath, personal preferences and beliefs, and perceptions of the public interest writ large.

For a responsible democratic citizen, knowledge of religious beliefs and the political views that emanate from them or coexist with them is essential. This book contributes to that knowledge. It is based on a national survey of public opinion and poll of elite opinion (both conducted for the Williamsburg Charter), a community-based survey of public opinion in Washington, D.C., and focus groups in Washington and Chicago. Authors Ted Jelen and Clyde Wilcox synthesize public and elite opinion over a range of church and state issues. Their objective is to discern the impact of religiosity on politics. They focus specifically on the tension that the separate but coexistent institutions of church and state produce within the political order.

The authors describe a rich tapestry of religious pluralism in America and its various political manifestations. In a population that is sharply divided between those with secular and those with sectarian beliefs; in a society in which the proportion of religious fundamentalists has grown significantly in recent years; at a time when religious groups are well organized, take stands, communicate effectively, and have become a powerful force within political parties as well as among the general public; the description and analysis in this book makes an extremely important contribution to our understanding of politics and policy in the 1990s.

Stephen J. Wayne
Georgetown University

Preface and Acknowledgments

As we write this in early 1995, the U.S. Congress has a newly elected Republican majority. After the Republicans pass the major legislation promised in their "Contract with America," House Speaker Newt Gingrich has promised to consider a constitutional amendment permitting organized, "voluntary" prayer in public schools. Republicans argue that amending the Constitution is necessary because the U.S. Supreme Court has ruled several times that organized school prayer violates the establishment clause of the First Amendment to the Constitution.

Such reaction to the constitutional issues posed by religion in the United States is not unusual. In recent years, state and local legislatures have attempted to pass religiously oriented measures designed to provide for Bible reading in public schools, to teach "scientific creationism" as an alternative to evolution, and to allow the display of religious symbols on public property. It is often the case that apparently popular, and perhaps innocuous, acts of government are prohibited as violations of the Constitution.

This is a book about public attitudes toward church–state relations. This topic assumes a central role in contemporary American politics for two reasons: First, Americans are very religious. Relative to other industrialized countries, religious belief and religious observance exist at very high levels. Second, religion and politics are separated as a matter of constitutional principle. As we will show, there is little agreement on the correct meanings of the religion clauses in the Constitution, but, at the level of general principles, few Americans would explicitly favor "establishing religion" or prohibiting religious "free exercise." Thus, religion is an important topic in American politics, but political conflict over religious beliefs and practices is conducted under unusual rules and constraints. The fact that religion is accorded special constitutional protection means that policy making in this area is often quite complicated. Further, the fact is that issues of constitutional interpretation are almost inevitably raised when government at any level attempts to make policy relevant to religion.

Why a book on public opinion in this area? Given the fact that so much church–state conflict takes place in the courts, it might reasonably be asked why, and to what extent, public opinion matters in these issues. The source of most law on the establishment and free-exercise clauses is the U.S. Supreme Court, which is insulated from public opinion. Federal judges are not elected; they are appointed for life. Thus, the relationship (if any) between public opinion and public policy in the area of church–state relations is likely to be indirect.

We believe that public opinion is important in these matters for several reasons. First, there are obvious ways in which the federal courts *are* political institutions. The process by which Supreme Court justices are selected is incorrigibly political. The recruitment of justices to the Supreme Court has been at least a minor campaign issue in presidential elections since 1968. To some extent, the prospect of appointing judges of particular ideological stripes guides the vote decisions of at least a few voters. Moreover, the process by which prospective members of the Court are confirmed by the Senate is occasionally quite ideological. For example, no one who followed the confirmation hearings of Robert Bork could in any candor deny that his rejection as a Supreme Court justice was motivated in large part by policy-related considerations or that Bork's public skepticism about a constitutional right to privacy was an important consideration in the final Senate vote (Bork 1990; Savage 1993). Despite an often stated norm that "excellence" is the only relevant criterion in judicial selection, "extraneous" political considerations are often decisive.

Moreover, many analysts have suggested that sitting justices are not immune to the political environment in which they operate. While the old adage that the Supreme Court follows the election returns may be overstated, most analysts of judicial behavior agree that the Court is not completely removed from the day-to-day operation of the political system. In their opinion in *Planned Parenthood of Southeastern Pennsylvania v. Casey,* Justices David Souter, Sandra Day O'Connor, and

Anthony Kennedy declined to overturn directly the precedent in *Roe v. Wade,* explaining that reversing such an important decision would cause the Court to be regarded as a "political" (in a pejorative sense) institution and would undermine the Court's legitimacy (Savage 1993).

Souter's unusually candid admission is evidence of something that political scientists have long suspected: The Court is sensitive to public opinion, and members of the Supreme Court may occasionally alter their behavior to conform to popular sentiment (see also Kluger 1977). While the extent of such sensitivity is controversial, and certainly would vary from justice to justice (and from issue to issue), no one would deny that the Court is often affected by the shadow cast by the more "political" branches of government. The relationship between public opinion and Supreme Court rulings is undoubtedly indirect, complex, and controversial, but few would argue that it does not exist.

Public opinion in church–state relations is important for another reason. Supreme Court rulings are not self-executing—that is, the Supreme Court cannot implement its own decisions but must reply on other branches of government. Moreover, the Court may not be able to correct whatever wrongs it may find but must confine itself to deciding the cases brought before it. Although the precise nature of the Court's discretion is controversial, some have argued that the Court is a passive institution in that it has limited control over its own agenda. When coupled with the fact that any aspect of constitutional law is necessarily incomplete, the Court's limited jurisdiction implies that a great deal of public policy relating to the political role of religion will inevitably be made outside the courts. Governmental units seeking to "establish" religion in some way, or to inhibit the free-exercise rights of religious minorities, may seek loopholes in the rules of law created by the courts (of which there are many), or they may simply ignore previous Supreme Court rulings. If dissenters lack the resources to utilize the court system (indeed, access to the federal court system is far from unlimited), there may exist substantial gaps between the "law" as enunciated by the courts and the actions of elected officials.

Third, the Supreme Court itself appears to be enhancing the importance of public opinion in church–state relations. The Rehnquist Court is increasingly deferential to the elected branches of government. Some argue that the Court is now more "accommodationist" with respect to issues involving religious establishment, and most see a pronounced move toward a more "communitarian" ethos in free-exercise cases. Indeed, it is perhaps noteworthy that Congress (an elected branch of government) is considering reinstating the "compelling state interest" standard of government restriction of free exercise to "correct" a decision of a Court deferential to the acts of elected branches of government. To the extent that the Supreme Court conducts itself in a more restrained manner, and allows greater latitude to elected officials in policy making of this type, decisions about appropriate and inappropriate relations between the sacred and the secular will be made in Congress and in state legislatures. As control of church–state controversies passes to the "popular" branches of government, the importance of public opinion about the religion clauses is likely to become even more important.

Finally, public opinion matters because publicly elected branches of government hold the ultimate authority over questions of constitutional interpretation: the power of constitutional amendment. In the contemporary political environment, Supreme Court rulings concerning the constitutionality of school prayer are extremely unpopular. These rulings can be definitively overridden by amending the Constitution to permit prayer in public schools. The Constitution, after all, cannot be unconstitutional. To amend the Constitution, extraordinary majorities are required in both houses of the U.S. Congress, and thirty-eight of the fifty state legislatures must approve[1] this process, the judiciary has no formal role to play at all, and members of the various legislatures can be expected to represent the will of popular majorities. Thus, public opinion is, in the final analysis, the court of final appeal in church–state relations.

What might we expect the shape of public opinion to be on these issues? As we will show in the text of this book, there are some analysts who regard the main axis of political conflict in the United States to be between the very religious and the not so religious. It may be that public opinion will be divided into proreligion and antireligion camps. Conversely, we might anticipate that divisions in public opinion will depend on the type of religious issue being raised. Most litigation involving the establishment clause has involved Christian symbols and activities: Christian prayers in schools, the reading of the Christian Bible, or the display of Christian symbols on public property. Therefore, we might expect devout Christians to support a relatively permissive (what we will call an "accommodationist") reading of the establishment clause. By contrast, most litigation related to the free-exercise clause has involved the claims of small and socially unusual religious minorities: Santerians seeking to practice animal sacrifice, Hare Krishnas seeking to solicit money and converts at airports, or Native Americans hoping to protect their rights to use hallucinogenic drugs for religious purposes. We might anticipate that support for such free-exercise claims would be most enthusiastic among groups who regard themselves as minorities or as the victims of discrimination.

In any event, we regard the subject matter of this book as being quite important for contemporary American politics. Religious issues are assuming increasing importance on the political agenda of the United States, and in a democracy such as ours, we believe that public opinion is ultimately an irresistible force.

Acknowledgments

We are grateful to the Williamsburg Charter Foundation for commissioning the national survey which we used as one of the major sources for this study, and for allowing us to use the data. A number of people have read and commented on various portions of this book, and their comments have produced a better book. We would like to thank Mary Bendyna, Richard Brisbin, Clarke Cochrane, Robert Katzmann, and Robin Wolpert for helpful comments. Susan Lagon also provided helpful suggestions. Our editor, Michael Weber, provided suggestions and encouragement.

William J. Wilcox served as a springboard for many of the ideas in this book, and his insights were particularly valuable in crafting the project. Over a number of years he was a constant source of ideas, and without his unflagging interest the project would not have been completed. We regret that he did not live to see the book completed, and we dedicate the book to his memory.

Ted G. Jelen
Clyde Wilcox

Note

1. It is also within the authority of state legislatures to require extraordinary majorities to pass constitutional amendments. For example, the Equal Rights Amendment was defeated in the Illinois legislature because of a requirement that amendments to the U.S. Constitution pass by a three-fifths majority.

1

Religion, Politics, and the Constitution

In the summer of 1994, the U.S. Supreme Court ruled that a New York state school district created for the benefit of the disabled children of Hasidic Jews was unconstitutional. In a 6–3 vote, the Court ruled in *Board of Education of Kiryas Joel Village School District v. Grumet* that such a school district violated the establishment clause of the Constitution (Biskupic 1994; Greenhouse 1994). Writing for the Court's majority, David Souter wrote that the legislature had created "a fusion of governmental and religious functions" and that government is required to demonstrate " 'neutrality' among religions" (Biskupic 1994, A1). Souter argued that the establishment clause requires that "government should not prefer one religion to another, or religion to irreligion" (Greenhouse 1994, A1).

In a biting dissent, Antonin Scalia mocked Souter's reasoning, arguing: "The Court today finds that the Powers that be, up in Albany, have conspired to affect an establishment of the Satmar Hasidim. . . . The Founding Fathers would be astonished to find that . . . the Court has abandoned text and history as guides . . . [and] nothing prevents it from calling religious toleration the establishment of religion" (Greenhouse 1994, D22).

In response to Scalia's dissent, Souter replied: "The license he [Scalia] takes in suggesting that the Court holds the Satmar sect to be New York's established church is only one symptom of his inability to accept the fact that this Court has long held that the First Amendment reaches more than classic, 18th-century establishments" (Greenhouse 1994, D21).

This unusually personal exchange between Supreme Court justices illustrates clearly that protagonists in the debate over the proper relationship between religion and government disagree fundamentally on a variety of issues. What is ultimately at stake are the meaning of the First Amendment to the Constitution and the proper role of religion in American public life. Such issues clearly have the capacity to provoke intensive, hyperbolic reactions and rhetoric. For more than half a century, the manner in which Americans "render unto Caesar the things which are Caesar's, and to God the things which are God's" (Matt. 22:21) has been a rich source of political and legal conflict in the United States.

The constitutional source of this conflict is sixteen words that begin the First Amendment to the U.S. Constitution:

"Congress shall make no law respecting an establishment of religion, or prohibiting the free exercise thereof. . . . " The precise meaning of these two clauses of the First Amendment (generally called the establishment clause and the free-exercise clause, respectively) has vexed scholars, lawyers, and citizens alike for a number of years. The sparse language of the U.S. Constitution has occasioned a massive volume of legal and scholarly writing and much disagreement and controversy in academic and legal circles.

Although the meaning of the First Amendment language on religious establishment and free exercise is ultimately decided by the U.S. Supreme Court, it is also debated in the electoral arena. Many Republican (and some Democratic) candidates for state and national office have staked positions in support of more public displays of Christian imagery and language, in part to attract conservative evangelical Christians that have increasingly become an important part of their constituencies. State legislatures have frequently passed laws designed to circumvent Supreme Court rulings on school prayer and Bible reading, and members of those legislatures have run for reelection claiming credit for such measures. It is likely that there will be a highly publicized debate on church–state issues in 1995 as the new Congress considers a constitutional amendment to allow prayer in public schools.

Moreover, there is evidence that the public cares about many of these issues. Debates about religious symbols in public schools or at Christmas arouse strong emotions among many American citizens, as do issues involving the rights of religious minorities. There is reason to believe, therefore, that many citizens will have relatively coherent and often intense positions on issues relating to church–state relations. This is not to say, of course, that the average American has spent much time considering many of the concrete issues of religious establishment or free exercise that the Supreme Court has decided. Yet we will show in later chapters that the public orders their beliefs on these issues in a meaningful fashion and that their attitudes are explained by their political, religious, and demographic characteristics.

This book is about the attitudes of the American public concerning issues of church–state relations. As such, it is not a legal or polemical work, nor is it a work of advocacy. We do not seek to take sides in the frequent debates over issues of church and state but only to examine and illuminate public opinion on these issues. Our purpose in this chapter is to offer a brief description and explanation of the political and legal context in which such matters are debated.

Most of this debate has centered on the proper interpretation of the establishment clause, which has been the center of more litigation and legislation than the free-exercise clause. In general, the resulting legal and academic controversies have generated two opposing camps, usually termed "accommodationists" and "separationists." Proponents of each position differ profoundly about the "correct" constitutional meaning of the establishment and free-exercise clauses and the role of religion in American public life.

Accommodationism and the Establishment Clause

Some analysts have suggested that the proper relationship between government and religion is one of "benevolent neutrality" (Wald 1992). They have suggested that government should pursue a policy that is generally favorable toward organized religion but that does not involve any preference for any particular religion. This orientation, usually termed "accommodationism" (Wald 1992) or "nonpreferentialism" (Levy 1986), is based upon two important assumptions about the political nature of religious belief.

First, accommodationists tend to assume that religion has beneficial consequences for human behavior; that is, religion provides a transcendent basis for morality and provides limits for the scope of political conflict. For example, A. James Reichley (1985), after reviewing a number of different ethical systems, concluded that only "theist-humanism" combines an objective, nonarbitrary basis for public morality with respect for the dignity and autonomy of each individual. Such a theological system (of which the Judeo-Christian tradition is a prime example) balances the need for public order with a respect for individual liberty.

Second, accommodationists tend to assume that, at bottom, most *Christian* religious traditions have similar political effects. Many analysts (see, for example, Kirk 1986) have cited Alexis de Tocqueville approvingly on the political consequences of Christianity in the United States: "The sects that exist in the United States are innumerable. They all differ in respect to the worship which is due to the Creator; but they all agree in respect to the duties which are due from man to man. . . . Moreover, all the sects of the United States are comprised within *the great unity of Christianity, and Christian morality is everywhere the same.* . . . Christianity, therefore, reigns without obstacle, by universal consent; the consequence is . . . that every principle of the moral world is fixed and determinate, although the political world is abandoned to the debates and experiments of men. . . ." (Tocqueville 1945, 314–15; emphasis added).

Thus, Tocqueville argued that the apparent diversity of American religion conceals a broad consensus on the behavioral consequences of religion. Whatever diversity exists among American Christians is confined to matters of doctrine and ritual (what some have called the "First Table" of the Ten Commandments) and does not extend to the duties that people owe one another. Religion is thought to fulfill a "priestly" function of legitimation of political authority (Jelen 1991b; Leege and Kellstedt 1993). Thus, a "Judeo-Christian tradition" is thought to provide the ethical basis of public life or what Peter Berger (1967) and Richard Neuhaus (1984) have termed a "sacred canopy" within which political affairs can be conducted.[1]

As Neuhaus elaborated: "Politics derives its directions from the ethos, from the cultural sensibilities that are the context of political action. The cultural context is shaped by our moral judgments and intuitions about how the world is and how it ought to be. Again, for the great majority of Americans such moral judgments and intuitions are inseparable from religious belief. Perhaps this is true not just of the majority but of all of us, whether or not we call our ultimate values religious. In any event, whether it is called the Judeo-Christian ethic, or Christianity, . . . it is the dynamic of religion that holds the promise of binding together *[religare]* a nation in a way that may more nearly approximate *civitas*" (1984, 60).

Given the assumption of a consensus on the ethical dimensions of religious faith, and the accommodationist belief in the positive effects of religion on political life, a certain view of the religion clauses of the Constitution follows. Accommodationists tend to take a very narrow view of the establishment clause, arguing that this clause *only* requires nonpreferentialism (Cord 1982; Wald 1992; Bradley 1987; Levy 1986). According to this view, government may not enact policies that favor one particular denomination over another, but there is no constitutional violation if government were to aid all religions impartially. Such policies as aid to parochial schools, tuition tax credits for private education, and nonsectarian school prayer are all considered constitutional by accommodationists, provided such policies are applied equally to all religions. Indeed, this view of the establishment clause may be considered the defining characteristic of the accommodationist position.

Separationism and the Establishment Clause

In contrast to the accommodationist emphasis on religious or cultural consensus, constitutional scholars within the tradition of "separationism" have tended to emphasize the diverse and divisive characteristics of American religion. Religious belief, it is argued, makes absolutist claims on the believer, which are not amenable to compromise (see Wald 1992). Far from being a source of social cohesion, religion is regarded as a source of much bitter political conflict. In his classic *Federalist #10,* James Madison listed differences in religion as a fertile source of "faction," which the Constitution is designed to control (Hamilton, Madison, and Jay 1937).[2] In a somewhat more humorous vein, Finley Peter Dunne's fictional Mr. Dooley made essentially the same point:

"Rellijon is a quare thing. Be itself it's all right. But sprinkle a little pollyticks into it an' dinnymit is bran flour compared with it. Alone it prepares a man f'r a better life. Combined with polyticks it hurries him to it" (quoted in Levy 1986, ix).

Given the potential volatility of religion as applied to political subjects, separationists view the purpose of the religion clauses of the First Amendment as depoliticizing religious belief. Religion is regarded as a dangerous element in democratic politics, one which is best confined to the private sphere of activity (Levy 1986; Pfeffer 1967).

Constitutionally, separationists take a broad view of the establishment clause, arguing that this portion of the First Amendment proscribes government involvement with religion in any form (Pfeffer
1967; Levy 1988). This expansive understanding of the establishment
clause was given the force of law in Hugo Black's opinion in *Everson
v. Board of Education* (1947): "The 'establishment of religion' clause
of the First Amendment means at least this: Neither a state nor the
Federal government can set up a church. Neither can pass laws which
aid one religion, *aid all religions,* or prefer one religion over another. . . .
No tax in any amount, large or small, can be levied to support any
religious activities or institutions, whatever they may be called, or what
ever form they may adopt to teach or practice religion. . . . In the words
of Jefferson, the clause against establishment of religion by law was
intended to erect 'a wall of separation between church and state.' "
(Cord 1982, 18; emphasis added).[3]

Accommodationists regard this stark language as fundamentally
mistaken (Cord 1982; Reichley 1985) and, indeed, as pernicious.
Black's interpretation of the establishment clause would seem to proscribe any form of government assistance to religion, including symbolic aid. Government encouragement of religious belief is considered
to be forbidden, even if such assistance were favored by a large majority of the population.

Not surprisingly, some accommodationist analysts regard separationism as hostile to religion itself (Wald 1992). Indeed, one collection of
accommodationist essays bears the title *The Assault on Religion* (Kirk
1986). Although it is clearly true that a separationist position would be
appropriate for one who sought to minimize the impact of religious
belief on political life, many separationists are deeply religious men and
women who regard a very strict distance between religion and politics
as beneficial to both. The religious case for separationism involves the
claim that religion and politics each operate most effectively when their
mutual independence is maximized.

According to Garry Wills (1990), Thomas Jefferson's brand of
separationism was designed precisely to enhance the moral authority
of religion. Jefferson (whose private correspondence is the source of
the phrase "wall of separation") believed that "true" religion—the sort
that satisfied the spiritual needs of the parishioners—required no governmental support. Only religions that were "false" or ineffective
needed assistance from outside the congregation. If denominations or

congregations were required to rely on their own resources, only those who actively attended to the needs and desires of their members would survive.

This argument is based on the metaphor of the economic marketplace. A "free market" in religion, like its economic counterpart, will produce pastors with strong incentives to satisfy their religious "customers." In recent years, a number of contemporary social scientists have made this economic analogy more explicit. Several studies (Iannaccone 1990; Finke 1990; Stark and McCann 1993; Finke and Stark 1992) have shown that competition between denominations (which is enhanced by a lack of governmental support of religion) increases the "supply" of religious "commodities" (number of churches, availability of clergy), as well as the extent of religious observance (for a critique of this more recent literature, see Bruce 1993). Thus, there exists a proreligion separationist argument to the effect that nonsupport of religion (perhaps paradoxically) creates the very environment in which a variety of religions can flourish.

Moreover, some separationists have argued that religion has an important political role to play, which is enhanced by independence between church and state. In a religiously pluralistic society, religion is often thought to have a prophetic function of moral and social critic (Jelen 1991b; Leege and Kellstedt 1993; Tinder 1989). Governments are run by men and women, who from the standpoint of most religious traditions are imperfect and prone to error. Religion's prophetic stance involves holding political actors accountable to standards imposed from outside the secular realm of politics. This critical position is arguably easier to maintain if religious bodies do not depend either directly or indirectly on government support. A natural reluctance to "bite the hand that feeds" might inhibit the ability of religious leaders to act as independent watchdogs on the political process.

The Free-Exercise Clause

Although most of the scholarly and political debate in the United States has focused on the establishment clause, there has been a good deal of litigation and controversy about free exercise as well. Although there is broad agreement that citizens whose religious beliefs fall into the Judeo-Christian tradition may worship privately, there has been considerable disagreement on whether these protections apply to unpopular religious minorities and to what extent religious practice deserves special protection by government.

Reichley (1985) made a distinction between "communitarian" and "libertarian" views of free exercise. In the communitarian view, the scope of legitimate free exercise is determined by popularly elected branches of government, such as state and local legislatures, which can limit the religious behaviors of religious minorities if they wish. For libertarians, however, religious free exercise must be allowed for nearly all religious groups.

While religious *beliefs* are considered inviolate by both communitarians and libertarians, a communitarian view of religious *conduct* permits people to act on their religious convictions as long as such actions do not offend the religious or moral views of the majority, as embodied in law. The libertarian view, in contrast, would allow religious activity so long as it does not clash with other fundamental rights. Thus, communitarians might allow a community to ban the worship of Satan because it offends the sensibilities of Christians while libertarians would allow that worship so long as it did not involve such pernicious practices as human sacrifice.

The communitarian view of free exercise qualifies substantially the notion that the free exercise of religion is an inalienable "right" (Brisbin 1992), but it is quite consistent with the assumption of the ethical consensus that underlies most versions of the accommodationist position on establishment. If an important characteristic of religion in the United States is agreement on certain fundamental rules of conduct, religious citizens who fall outside such a consensus pose a problem for the political culture.

Indeed, journalist and sometime presidential candidate Pat Buchanan has suggested that immigration into the United States should be restricted selectively, depending on whether prospective immigrants come from countries compatible with fundamental principles of our "American," Judeo-Christian culture (Morganthau 1993). As Buchanan put it: "When we say we will put America first, we mean also that our Judeo-Christian values are going to be preserved and our Western heritage is going to be handed down to future generations and not dumped into some landfill called multiculturalism. . . . I think God made all people good, but if we were to take a million immigrants in, say Zulus, next year, or Englishmen, and put them in Virginia, what group would be easier to assimilate and cause less problems for the people of Virginia?" (Germond and Witcover 1993, 136).

By contrast, a libertarian view of the free-exercise clause would entail granting broad latitude to a variety of unconventional religious practices. Such a broad view of the free-exercise clause would, in principle, create a presumption that members of religious "cults," such as Satanists or "Moonies," or adherents of non-Western religions are allowed to engage in religious practices that most Americans would regard as bizarre or repugnant. The argument underlying such a permissive reading of the free-exercise clause is a version of a "slippery slope" analogy. If government is permitted to regulate unconventional or unpopular religious practices, the day may come when government seeks to restrict more conventional religions. Once the principle of government restriction of free exercise is established, it is difficult to see how the process might be limited.

Tensions between the Establishment and Free-Exercise Clauses

Of course, some issues span the interstitial zone between establishment and free exercise. Consider, for example, the question of whether a school district should allow a moment of silence for prayer, meditation, or other thoughts. Most separationists would see this as an establishment issue, involving a back-door attempt to reinstitute prayer in schools. Some religious groups, however, argue that the issue is instead one of free exercise for it involves the right of children to pray. Or consider the question of whether state universities should provide space and funding for student religious newspapers. Ironically, there is a case on just this issue pending at Thomas Jefferson's own University of Virginia.[4]

Some free-exercise claims ask the government to use its positive power to free them from certain responsibilities: the responsibility to fight in wars or to work on the Sabbath. Such claims can also be seen as involving religious establishment, for to honor these claims the government would be helping a specific religious group. They can also be seen as promoting the free exercise of religious belief. These examples demonstrate that many issues involve both the free-exercise and establishment clauses, which are potentially in conflict.

Among accommodationists, there is disagreement on the scope of coverage of the free-exercise clause but consensus that the establishment and free-exercise clauses are not in conflict, at least in the case of

Christian religious exercise. Most accommodationists believe that free-exercise claims may require positive action by government to exempt citizens from some requirements or to provide them with special services.

For example, local governments now routinely provide free compulsory public education for children. While it is widely accepted that parents may send their children to private (often religious) schools, the precise conditions under which governments can provide assistance to such sectarian institutions, or to the parents of such children, are as yet unclear.

Accommodationists argue that the parents of parochial-school students are faced with what amounts to a "double taxation"; that is, their taxes support the public schools (of which they do not take direct advantage) while they must pay tuition to keep their children in religious schools. Such financial constraints might be considered interference with the free-exercise rights of such parents because government tax policies impose costs on the assertion of religious liberty (in this instance, the right to educate one's children within the faith). Yet separationists see a dilemma here for protecting this freedom requires government assistance to religion.

To an accommodationist, this is a false dilemma, occasioned by an overly expansive view of the establishment clause. The accommodationist position can accept such a broad reading of the free-exercise clause because all the establishment clause is considered to require is impartiality among religions. If tax incentives are available to students in all religious schools, accommodationists see no constitutional violation (for an overview and analysis of this issue, see Reichley 1985). The accommodationist view of the religion clauses of the First Amendment thus suggests that the establishment and free-exercise clauses are generally consistent and mutually supportive. Many accommodationists would argue that the free-exercise clause is indeed the more important of the religion clauses and that the primary purpose of the establishment clause is to protect free exercise from government policies preferential to particular religions (Monsma 1993a).

Separationists are more likely to perceive conflict between the two clauses. For example, Black's *Everson* opinion would seem to impose substantial limits on the free-exercise clause. Black's prohibition on the use of tax revenue to support religion "in whatever form" implies that free-exercise claims will not be taken seriously when applied to the positive benefits of activist government; that is, a claim of free exercise cannot, from a separationist standpoint, be used to justify a demand for government services or relief from public obligations.

Consider the private-school tax voucher example from above. From the viewpoint of a separationist, *any* government support for religion (including relief from an alleged burden of double taxation) constitutes an unconstitutional "establishment" of religion. Therefore, such credits, vouchers, or deductions cannot be justified, whatever the collateral damage to claims of "free exercise." Separationists argue that parents who send their children to religious schools do not face double taxation for they are merely purchasing goods privately that are also provided by government. Like wealthy citizens who choose to hire private security guards to protect their property while paying taxes to support the police, parents who choose private religious schools must support the public system while opting for additional private services.

The separationist position strongly suggests that the establishment clause is the most important and that free-exercise claims cannot demand positive government support in light of a stringent interpretation of religious "establishment." In the voucher example, separationists might wonder whether such tax incentives would violate the antiestablishment rights of nonreligious people or of members of denominations too small to support their own schools. One might also be skeptical of the willingness of an elected legislature to provide even indirect financial support to unconventional religions lying outside a "Judeo-Christian" mainstream.

Some accommodationists, in contrast, argue that the free-exercise clause is the most important and that the separationist view of the establishment clause constricts the correct meaning of the free-exercise clause. Because accommodationists value the general role of religion in American public life, such a limitation of free exercise is most unfortunate. As Monsma (1993a; 1993b) has suggested, maximizing the free exercise of religion often involves offering assistance to religion. To restrict government assistance offered to nonreligious agents on the basis of running afoul of the establishment clause is, from the standpoint of accommodationists, restricting free exercise (see also Neuhaus 1992; and Carter 1993).

Points of Contention

Clearly there is a great deal of disagreement over the proper purpose and scope of the religion clauses of the First Amendment. The literature on the general topic of church–state relations in the United States is enormous, and the study of the proper relationship between God and Caesar has been well institutionalized in American scholarship. There is at least one academic journal *(The Journal of Church and State)* primarily devoted to First Amendment issues, and Baylor University has established an Institute of Church–State Studies. Such well-established intellectual structures demonstrate that the disputes over church–state relations have long pedigrees and will be with us for some time to come. In this section, our intention is simply to provide a flavor of the types of arguments made by accommodationist and separationist analysts while making absolutely no pretense of solving any of the issues involved. The material in this chapter is only intended to be illustrative: Readers interested in pursuing any of the issues raised here in more detail are referred to a number of excellent works listed in the reference list.

An obvious starting point in determining the "correct" meaning of the religion clauses of the First Amendment is to look at the wording of the amendment itself. Presumably, an analyst who sought the meaning of a particular constitutional provision would begin by reading the text in question. Unfortunately, this sort of textual exegesis has not settled any of the outstanding questions, nor has such analysis narrowed the range of intellectually permissible interpretations.

This kind of analysis sometimes focuses on a single word. For example, some accommodationists have argued that the article employed in the establishment clause clearly supports an interpretation of non-preferentialism (see Malbin 1978). Because the establishment clause proscribes *an* establishment of religion, and not *the* establishment of religion, the clause is taken to prohibit particular establishments but not a more general establishment. The use of the particular article is thus thought to imply that general assistance to religion is constitutionally permitted. However, Levy (1986) has suggested that whatever the merits of the choice of article in the establishment clause, the clause prohibits Congress from making any law *respecting* the establishment of religion. Levy's argument is that rather than simply prohibit religious establishments of whatever nature, the establishment clause proscribes Congress from making any law relating to religious establishment in any way whatsoever.

Levy also argued that this sort of close textual analysis is a double-edged sword. He suggested that the First Amendment prevents Congress from making any law *prohibiting* the free exercise of religion or making any law *abridging* freedom of speech or press. Given a literal interpretation of these verbs, it might well be argued that the rights of free speech and press are more carefully protected than the right of free exercise because government presumably is allowed to make laws "abridging" but not "prohibiting" the free exercise of religion.

This type of grammatical analysis has generally been inconclusive, owing to the broad nature of constitutional language and, perhaps, to the mixed motives of those conducting these studies. Therefore, some analysts have suggested that scholars who seek the "authentic" meaning of constitutional provisions look to the intentions of the framers of the Constitution or to those of the authors of particular amendments. The battle over "original intent" has been a heated one among lawyers and constitutional scholars throughout American history and seems to have reached a particular intensity during the Reagan administration. Bork (1990) has suggested that the only valid interpretive rule for understanding the Constitution is to attempt to understand, as accurately as possible, the intentions of the people who wrote the document. Any other gloss, argued Bork, is to substitute the subjective bias of the judge for the "true" meaning of the Constitution.

By contrast, other analysts have argued that the Constitution can and should be interpreted in light of contemporary meanings and usages (see especially Tribe and Dorf 1991). There are, according to this viewpoint, intermediate limitations of permissible constitutional analysis that do not involve either freezing the meaning of the document to the time it was written or accepting unrestricted subjectivity on the part of contemporary judges (for an overview of the nature of original intent as applied to the religion clauses, see Wood 1990). Further, the specific intentions of the framers of the Constitution or of subsequent amendments may be difficult to discern because different writings and utterances may be offered with different rhetorical purposes (see Lindsay 1991). Editorials, or speeches delivered to a legislative body, may contain varying levels of candor or may be tailored to the characteristics of a particular audience.

Despite the fact that the authority of original intent is *not* a settled principle of constitutional interpretation, both accommodationists and separationists have devoted enormous resources to determining the intentions of the authors of the Bill of Rights. As was the case with textual analysis, the search for the historical meanings of the religion clauses of the First Amendment has not been conclusive.

Scholars of both accommodationist and separationist perspectives have sought to illuminate the framers' original intent with respect to the religion clauses. In the most general sense, some accommodationists have pointed out that many of the framers were deeply religious and believed that politics required a moral and religious basis (see especially Reichley 1985). More specifically, accommodationists have argued that the term "establishment" had a clear, unambiguous meaning in the 1790s. Establishment was, in these accounts, thought to mean the designation and support of an official, government-sponsored denomination (Curry 1986). In the United States, several states had established religions in this narrow sense of the word (Curry 1986; Cord 1982). Thus, some would argue that the term "establishment" had a narrow, agreed-upon meaning that referred specifically to nonpreferentialism and *only* to nonpreferentialism.

Some accommodationists have also made reference to the legislative debate surrounding congressional adoption of the First Amendment. They have suggested that Madison's original formulation of the establishment clause (proscribing a "national religion") supports a nonpreferentialist perspective (Cord 1982; Bradley 1987). The resulting revision, it is argued, was intended to smooth over differences over the proper scope of federal authority (e.g., some supporters of the new Constitution would not acknowledge that the Constitution had, in fact, created a "national" government).

Finally, supporters of a nonpreferentialist interpretation of the establishment clause point to a variety of accommodationist acts by Presidents Madison (an important figure in the writing of the original Constitution, as well as the First Amendment) and Jefferson (the source of much historical "separationist" rhetoric). Madison revived the Federalist practice of Presidents Washington and Adams of proclaiming national Days of Thanksgiving, in which citizens were encouraged to thank their Creator for His blessings. While President Jefferson had discontinued this practice, he consistently provided funding for Catholic missionaries to minister to Native-American tribes (Cord 1982; Bradley 1987).[5] Thus, it is argued that the framers whose views on the establishment clause were most conspicuous appear to have had a narrow, nonpreferentialist understanding of the First Amendment.

However, some histories of the enactment of the establishment clause support a separationist perspective. In general, separationists who characterize the religious beliefs of the founders emphasize the eclectic diversity of these beliefs, including the rather unconventional theologies of such luminaries as Jefferson and Benjamin Franklin (Wills 1990).

Separationists also offer more specific historical arguments concerning the meaning of the establishment clause. Levy (1986; 1988) has argued that the term "establishment" was not free of ambiguity at the time of the enactment of the First Amendment. A number of states had multiple establishments in which government directly supported more than one denomination. Some states had the equivalent of "home rule" provisions in which local governments could determine which denomination(s) they wished to support. Levy reported that a number of newspaper articles in New England were quite critical of the decision of the Canadian government to establish both Roman Catholicism and Anglicanism because such a policy "established Romanism." Thus, some analysts have argued that the notion of a multiple establishment was quite familiar to some politically active citizens in the 1790s (the practice appears to have been most common in New England) and that the establishment clause can plausibly be read to prohibit this more general type of establishment.

Analysts of the legislative history of the First Amendment have also suggested that some of the evidence supports a separationist perspective. It has been argued (Levy 1986; Curry 1986) that although Madison's initial draft of the First Amendment contained non-preferentialist language, he ultimately withdrew this version, substituting the more general language that was eventually adopted. Moreover, the Senate considered three different versions of the First Amendment that contained explicitly nonpreferentialist language and rejected all three (Levy 1986; 1988). Thus, if legislative votes are valid indicators of the intentions of members of Congress, some evidence suggests that Congress considered, and rejected, nonpreferentialism (see also Wood 1990).

It has also been argued that the writings of prominent commentators on the First Amendment, such as Madison and Jefferson, may support a separationist position as well. As noted above, accommodationists point to Madison's Thanksgiving proclamations as evidence of his approval of generalized support for religion. However, in Madison's "Detached Memoranda," written in retirement in 1817, he expressed regret for having engaged in this practice, adding that such general support for religion "probably" violated the establishment clause (see Fleet 1946; Wills 1990; Levy 1986).

Apart from such historical minutiae, Levy (1986) approached the First Amendment from a more general perspective. He argued that the framers understood the Constitution to be creating a government limited to only those powers that are expressly granted to it. The federal government, it is argued, was not considered to have any powers not specifically created in the original Constitution. It is this assumption that is made explicit in the Ninth and Tenth Amendments in the Bill of Rights.[6] Because the original Constitution does not grant the federal government any jurisdiction in the area of religion, it must be inferred that the federal government has none.

Levy went on to argue that if the establishment clause has a non-preferentialist meaning, this would have the effect of creating a positive power for the federal government; that is, nonpreferentialism would suggest that Congress is in fact empowered to legislate in the area of religious practice, as long as it does not favor a particular religion. This argument implies that the establishment clause empowers the federal government in a general way by granting it permission to legislate in religious matters. Levy argued that such an interpretation is entirely inconsistent with the purpose of the Bill of Rights, which consists of a series of *limitations* on the power of the federal government. Thus, an accommodationist reading of the First Amendment may be inconsistent with the spirit of the Bill of Rights taken as a whole.[7]

This massive and contentious literature on the meaning of the religion clauses of the First Amendment has not produced anything approaching a consensus on the meaning of the free-exercise or (especially) the establishment clause. What, then, should be done if agreement on the unique meaning or intentions of the framers cannot be ascertained? Here again, there are important differences. Because accommodationists tend to emphasize the integrative, consensual aspects of religion, the accommodationist position suggests that judges should defer to popularly elected legislatures, except where the most egregious violations are concerned (see especially Bork 1990). Legislatures, after all, are directly accountable to public opinion in ways that federal judges (appointed for lifetime terms) are not. If the legislature makes a mistake, it can be rectified at the next election, whereas mistakes made by federal judges have a longer lifespan. Characterizing situations in which the "correct" meaning of the Constitution cannot be ascertained, Bork has written, "There being nothing to work with, the judge should refrain from working" (1990, 166). For judges to substitute their interpretations of the Constitution for the will of officials elected by popular majorities is to violate the norms of democracy and to impose rule by an unelected, oligarchic judiciary.

By contrast, separationists tend to emphasize the divisive, conflictual elements of religious belief and are thus fearful of the "tyranny of the majority" (Tocqueville 1945). Mary Ann Glendon (1991) has noted that implicit in the concept of a "right" is that rights are held beyond the reach of popular majorities. The "right" to free exercise of religion, or to be free from religious "establishment" (whatever these elusive terms might mean), should not depend on the prevailing mood or direction of public opinion. Indeed, people who hold unconventional or unpopular beliefs are thought to require protection from majority opinion. Separationists are extremely skeptical of the tendency of accommodationists to defer to elected branches of government, and they tend to regard the courts as a counterweight to potentially coercive tendencies of legislatures (Levy 1986; Wald 1992). Separationists tend to believe that federal judges should scrutinize the actions of popularly elected branches of government very carefully and base their rulings on a broad understanding of the establishment clause.

The State of the Law

In an important sense, it is easier to describe competing positions on what the law governing church–state relations *should* be than it is to summarize what the law actually *is*. In the United States, legal rules are often created by judicial decisions, which in turn *usually* (but not always) create precedents for future cases. Like other Anglo-American (English) systems of law, the American system is "open" (in that there is no comprehensive body of doctrine on which American law is based) and "inductive" (rules of law are settled on a case-by-case basis). The system is thus incomplete, in the sense that there are always many areas for which no specific rule of law exists, and is occasionally internally inconsistent (see David and Brierly 1978).

With these caveats in mind, it seems fair to characterize constitutional law as generally "separationist" with respect to the establishment clause. At this writing, the operative precedent remains *Lemon v.*

Kurtzman (1971), in which Chief Justice Warren Burger proposed a three-pronged test to determine whether a given government policy violates the establishment clause. The Lemon test would invalidate a particular government policy if that policy has a religious purpose, has the effect of advancing or inhibiting religion, *or* requires an "excessive entanglement" between government and religion (Wald 1992). Violation of any of these conditions is sufficient to render particular government policies unconstitutional. It should be emphasized that nothing in the Lemon test limits its application to policy toward *specific* denominations.

To illustrate the meaning of the "religious-purpose" prong of the Lemon test, the Supreme Court has struck down a Louisiana law that would have required public schools to devote "equal time" to the teaching of evolution and creationism (*Edward v. Aguillard*, 1987), as well as an Alabama measure mandating a "moment of silence" in public schools (*Wallace v. Jaffree*, 1985). In both of these cases, the Court held that the primary purpose of the legislation was to advance religious beliefs.

Similarly, the "effects" prong of the Lemon test suggests that governments might be permitted to assist religious institutions, provided the primary effect of the policy was secular in nature. For example, it might well be constitutional for a state government to provide mathematics textbooks to parochial schools because the state has a secular interest in promoting mathematics instruction. However, general state assistance to parochial schools (which would presumably benefit both secular and religious instruction) would be deemed unconstitutional (Wald 1992). Indeed, the Court struck down state and local measures on such a basis in *Abingdon Township School District v. Schempp* (1963), even before it articulated the Lemon test, and did so again in *Allegheny County v. ACLU* (1989) afterward.

The "entanglement" aspect of the Lemon test means that government policy should not involve religion in political activity to any "excessive" degree, nor should government be involved in intensive scrutiny of religious practice. To illustrate, it might well be constitutional for government to provide mathematics *textbooks* to students in parochial schools; it might not be permissible for the state to compensate mathematics *instructors*. The distinction is based on the probability that the state government would have to monitor the activities of math teachers rather frequently to ensure that the nature of the instruction remained secular and that no proscribed religious instruction was enhanced through government assistance.

Leo Pfeffer (1984) has suggested that instruction of even secular subjects such as mathematics in religious educational institutions might require extensive monitoring. He offered several examples of story problems (the bane of junior-high students from time immemorial) to illustrate this point:

> How much money must I have to buy these four books? *Poems About the Christ Child,* $1.85; *Story of Our Lady,* $2.25; *St. Joseph,* $1.05; *St. Theresa,* $2.00.

> The Children of St. Francis School ransomed 125 pagan babies last year. This year they hope to increase this number by 20%. If they succeed, how many babies will they ransom this year?

> Jim made the Way of the Cross. He likes the sixth station very much. What Roman numeral was written above it?

> China has a population of approximately 600,000,000. Through the efforts of missionaries, 3,000,000 have been converted to Catholicism. What percentage of the people of China have been converted? (Pfeffer 1984, 35–36)

Presumably, the Lemon test would proscribe this "indirect" form of religious instruction, even though addition, percentages, and Roman numerals are part of the legitimately secular subject of mathematics.

In recent years, the Supreme Court appears to be applying the Lemon test less stringently than previously although the *Lemon* precedent itself has not been overturned. In the 1992/93 term, the Court permitted state funding for a sign-language interpreter for a deaf student enrolled in a Catholic school *(Zobrest v. Catalina Foothills School District)* and required public schools to permit religious groups to use school facilities after hours if such use is extended to nonreligious groups *(Lamb's Chapel v. Center Moriches Union Free School District).* (For an overview of these cases from an accommodationist standpoint, see Kilpatrick 1993.) However, in the case of *Lee v. Weisman* (1992), the Court struck down "voluntary" prayer at a high-school graduation ceremony (Robbins 1993). In general, the Court appears to be moving very cautiously in an accommodationist direction without making major shifts in constitutional doctrine (Urofsky 1993).

In contrast to the generally separationist cast of Supreme Court decisions respecting religious establishment, the Court has generally taken a libertarian view toward free-exercise claims. Although the right to exercise one's religious beliefs has never been absolute (in 1879, the Court upheld a law prohibiting polygamy for Mormons in *Reynolds v. United States*), the Court has traditionally been quite sensitive to the prerogatives of nontraditional religious groups (Brisbin 1992). Some analysts have gone so far as to suggest that, until very recently, free-exercise jurisprudence has primarily benefited religious minorities (Way and Burt 1983).[8]

Thomas Robbins (1993) has suggested that the Supreme Court has historically adopted a three-part test for evaluating the constitutionality of free-exercise claims. These criteria were derived from the cases of *Sherbert v. Verner* (1963) and *Wisconsin v. Yoder* (1972). The first part of what Robbins termed the "Sherbert–Yoder balancing test" is the "compelling state interest" standard. Under this criterion, the government must show that "it has a compelling interest which justifies abridgment of the . . . right to free exercise of religion" (Pfeffer 1979, 2) and that such regulations will be subject to the "strict scrutiny" of the courts. This has proven to be a rather formidable hurdle for government policies. Indeed, the compelling state interest standard has traditionally required that government show a particular regulation to be practically *essential* to justify limiting free-exercise claims (Wald 1992).[9]

Once the centrality of the purpose of government regulation has been established, the Sherbert–Yoder test has traditionally examined the role of particular practices in the belief system of a particular religion. In order to be protected, a religious practice has to be "central" to the religion under consideration, and the government regulation in question had to result in a "substantial infringement" on the practice of that religion.

Finally, courts have traditionally considered whether an essential or compelling government regulation restricting free exercise is the least restrictive alternative by which the state might pursue its interest. If a government can achieve substantially the same purpose with a less intrusive policy, a particular regulation might well be deemed unconstitutional (see Wald 1992, 156, for illustrations of this principle).

The Court's traditional deference to free-exercise claims appears to be changing during the term of the Rehnquist Court. In *Employment Division v. Smith* (1990), the Court ruled that a Native-American religious ritual involving the use of the hallucinogenic drug peyote is not protected under the free-exercise clause. Writing for the Court's majority, Scalia argued that actions that would otherwise be prohibited under a state's criminal code are not accorded special protection under the First Amendment unless such exception is explicitly made by the legislature (Savage 1993). Under the *Smith* ruling, the Court appears to have moved away from the compelling state interest or "strict scrutiny" standard (Brisbin 1992). As such, the Court may be moving away from a libertarian understanding of the free-exercise clause to a more communitarian one. Consistent with the consensual nature of accommodationism, the Court in *Smith* may have signaled that it will accord the acts of legislatures (and, by extension, popular majorities) great deference.[10]

In response to the Court's ruling in *Smith,* Congress in 1993 passed a measure, popularly known as the Religious Freedom Restoration Act, which reinstates the compelling state interest standard. This measure has been supported by an unusual coalition of mainline Protestants, Southern Baptists, and Orthodox Jews, among others (see Hirsley 1993).

The Postwar Explosion of Court Decisions

For most of American history, the religion clauses of the First Amendment did not generate much in the way of controversy. Prior to 1940, there were no major church–state cases decided by the U.S. Supreme Court (Robbins 1993; Wald 1992). The Court began to consider church–state relations in the early 1940s, in the cases of *Cantwell v. Connecticut* (1940), *Minersville School District v. Gobitis* (1940), and *West Virginia State Board of Education v. Barnette* (1943). However, most of the litigation over the religion clauses of the First Amendment occurred in the aftermath of World War II (Reichley 1985; Robbins 1993). Indeed, the vast majority of cases involving church–state issues have been initiated during the past fifty years.[11]

There seem to be four principal reasons for the apparent explosion of First Amendment litigation in the postwar era. In the first place, the United States after World War II has been characterized by a much greater level of religious diversity than had previously been the case. For most of its history, the United States has primarily been a nation comprised of Protestants (Cord 1982). After the Civil War, several waves of Catholic and Jewish immigration challenged this Protestant social hegemony. In the most recent period, the United States has received immigrants who practice Islam, Buddhism, Hinduism, and other religions from outside the Judeo-Christian tradition. Moreover, Americans have had to consider the religious liberty of members of "cults" in recent years. Many Americans have regarded such people as Hare Krishnas, "Moonies," cult leaders such as David Koresh, and Satanists as lying outside the bounds of religious respectability, and some have been reluctant to extend full religious liberty to such unconventional beliefs (Robbins 1993). Such diversity of belief is important because principles of constitutional law are not, from a practical standpoint, self-executing. The Court must rely on other branches of government, at both the state and federal level, to implement its decrees. Moreover, the U.S. Supreme Court does not have a roving jurisdiction to correct wrongs wherever they might occur but is limited to deciding cases brought before it. If government at some level violates religious freedom in some manner but no one complains, the courts are powerless to act. The presence of a wide range of religious beliefs in the United States makes it much more likely that plaintiffs will exist in controversies regarding religious liberty.[12]

Second, government at all levels has dramatically increased the services it offers citizens and the taxation it charges citizens to pay for such services. As such, the modern (post–New Deal) American has much more interaction with government officials than her or his historical counterparts. The increase in affirmative government activity provides many more occasions in which possible violations of religious liberty might occur. For example, the questions of tuition tax credits or school prayer are unlikely to occur in a society in which government does not provide compulsory public education. Does a tax exemption for religious organizations constitute an unlawful establishment of religion, or are such exemptions necessary for believers to exercise fully their free-exercise rights? Similarly, the question of the legality of religiously based racial discrimination (as was posed in the *Bob Jones* cases) might not occur unless the elimination of race-based inequities is a government policy. In sum, more government provides more opportunities for church–state conflict (Robbins 1993). Indeed, a great many church–state issues deal with public education and would not pose constitutional questions were government not as actively involved in educational policy.

Third, the tactics of interest groups have, in some cases, involved a shifting of emphasis from legislatures to courts. At least since the landmark case of *Brown v. Board of Education* (1954), many organized groups have sought to have their grievances heard by the federal courts. Such a strategy has been particularly attractive if the group in question is a relatively small or unpopular minority. In such instances, many of these groups have found the courts more responsive than popularly elected legislatures (see especially Way and Burt 1983).

Finally, church–state conflict has increased in part because of the doctrine of "incorporation" (Levy 1986, 1988; Friendly and Elliot 1984). Strictly speaking, the Bill of Rights (including the religion clauses of the First Amendment) is a set of prohibitions on the powers of *Congress*. For much of American history, the Bill of Rights has been believed to limit the extent of the powers of the *federal* government but not those of government at the state or local level. Indeed, state establishments of religion, although uncommon, continued to exist for the first third of the nineteenth century (Levy 1988; Cord 1982).

The strict distinction between restrictions on the federal government and those on lower governmental levels has eroded steadily since the Civil War. In most instances, citizens of the United States now have the same rights with respect to all levels of government. State governments, as well as the federal government, are prohibited from abridging free speech, from imposing cruel and unusual punishment or from imposing unreasonable searches and seizures. Over a period of time, the Bill of Rights has gradually been "incorporated" to include state and local governments. Such incorporation began slowly with *Chicago, Burlington, and Quincy Railroad Co. v. Chicago* in 1897, and with *Gitlow v. New York* in 1925 (McDowell 1993) and has steadily been expanded to cover several of the first ten amendments.

The constitutional basis of incorporation is the "due-process" clause of the Fourteenth Amendment (ratified in 1868). The pertinent portion of the Fourteenth Amendment reads, "Nor shall any State deprive any person of life, liberty, or property, without due process of law. . . . " *Gradually,* this phrase has been interpreted to create national citizenship and to apply rights of the United States to all levels of government (see Kluger 1977).[13] Over a long period of time, the due-process clause, which is applicable to the states (not the federal government), has been interpreted to apply to the rights guaranteed by the Bill of

Rights. Therefore, the restrictions on the federal government imposed by the Bill of Rights are also restrictions that apply to the states.

The religion clauses were first applied to the actions of a state government in 1940 in *Cantwell v. Connecticut* and in 1947 in *Everson v. Board of Education* and have generally been applied to the actions of subnational governments ever since. The precise scope of the Fourteenth Amendment remains controversial (Friendly and Elliot 1984; McDowell 1993), and some recent analysts have suggested that its application to religious activity of state and local government is illegitimate (Reichley 1985; Kirk 1986). However, the extension of the religion clauses of the First Amendment to subnational units of government appears to be well established, and a challenge to the incorporation of the religion clauses probably would not be seriously considered by the Supreme Court.

Of course, the incorporation of the Bill of Rights into subnational jurisdictions increases drastically the potential for conflict over church–state issues. Most (but not all) church–state controversies involve the actions of state or local governments, such as education policies, holiday displays on public property, or Sabbath observances. Although one may not agree completely with Thomas P. "Tip" O'Neill's observation that "all politics is local," it seems to be the case that religion and politics have their most frequent contact at the local level.

Thus, the most recent period in American history has witnessed a large increase in political conflict in issues involving church–state relations. Nearly two centuries of relative political silence on the issue have ended abruptly, and the political role of religion now occupies a position near the center of American politics.

A Typology of Church–State Positions

There is no *necessary* relationship between positions on issues of religious establishment and free exercise. We have distinguished two distinctive positions on both the establishment and free-exercise clauses of the First Amendment. Of course, there are many subtle nuances to the actual positions of elites and the general public, and many Americans do not fall neatly into these groupings. We can nonetheless create from these categories a typology of possible combinations of positions on church–state issues. The typology is shown in Table 1.1.[14]

Table 1.1

A Typology of Church–State Positions

Free-Exercise Clause	Establishment Clause	
	Accomodationist	Separationist
Communist	Christian Preferentialist	Religious Minimalist
Libertarian	Religious Nonpreferentialist	Religious Free-Marketeer

Those who take accommodationist positions on the establishment clause can take either a communalist or a libertarian position on the free-exercise clause. We will refer to accommodationists who hold a communalist position on issues of free exercise as "Christian preferentialists" because they would not regard certain forms of government assistance to religion as violating the establishment clause and would also be willing to restrict at least some of the free-exercise prerogatives of groups falling outside the boundaries of a presumed cultural consensus. Such people might well believe that the United States is a "Christian nation" (or adheres to a Judeo-Christian tradition) in which popular majorities should be allowed to determine the relationship between God and Caesar. By contrast, accommodationists who take a libertarian position on free exercise we will call "religious nonpreferentialists" because they favor neutral government assistance and affirmation of religion but would allow all kinds of religious groups to participate in the public square.

Those who take separationist positions on the establishment clause can also take communalist or libertarian positions on the free-exercise clause. Those separationists who take a communalist position we will call "religious minimalists" because they apparently want to minimize the role of religion in public life. They may wish to limit religious free exercise to majority groups and to limit public support for religion. Such people might well argue that religiously based prerogatives deserve no special consideration and that government ought not provide any support for religious expression.

Those separationists who take a libertarian position on free exercise we will call "religious free-marketeers" for they favor allowing a variety of religious groups to compete for adherents while the government remains entirely neutral, not only among religious groups, but also between religion and irreligion. Such people believe that government should neither support nor restrict religious practice. In chapter 6, we will see if this typology of elite positions bears any relationship to the beliefs of the general public.

Conclusion

The general area of church–state relations is a rich source of political controversy. The sparse language of the religion clauses of the First Amendment has provided political, legal, and academic analysts with a great deal of ammunition for conflict concerning the proper constitutional role of religion in American politics.

The rest of this book is devoted to describing and explaining public attitudes toward the relationship between church and state. We will consider general and specific attitudes toward issues involving religious establishment, as well as those pertaining to free-exercise applications. The perspectives of ordinary citizens also will be examined and compared with those of political, educational, religious, business, and media elites.

Notes

1. Most accommodationists speak of a "Judeo-Christian tradition," arguing that a great portion of the ethical basis of Western religion is found in what Christians term the "Old Testament" or what Jews might call the "Hebrew Bible."

2. In *Federalist #10*, Madison regarded religion as a less potent source of faction than economic interests.

3. It should be noted that in *Everson* the Court upheld the constitutionality of a measure authorizing reimbursement of transportation costs to parents whose children attended parochial schools.

4. Anyone who has toured the University of Virginia campus will recall Jefferson's serpentine walls and can invent their own metaphors for this case.

5. A case can be made that such a practice would violate even a nonpreferentialist understanding of the establishment clause because it would involve funding for a specific denomination.

6. The Ninth Amendment states that the American people may have rights other than those listed in the Bill of Rights while the Tenth Amendment reserves all powers not specifically delegated to the federal government to the states or to the people.

7. As might be expected, arguments based on the "spirit" of the Constitution are themselves quite controversial. In the 1989 case of *Michael H. v. Gerald D.*, Scalia argued that rights must be characterized at the most specific level that can be identified. Thus, Scalia (among others) would likely regard the process of

examining the purpose of the entire Bill of Rights as illegitimate. See Tribe and Dorf (1991).

8. Of course, the Court's accommodationist view of free-exercise claims has not been uniform. See especially *U.S. v. Lee* (1982), *Heffron v. International Society for Krishna Consciousness* (1981), and *Goldman v. Weinberger* (1986) for instances in which the Court rejected an appellant's free-exercise claim.

9. The extent to which the compelling state interest test has been applied stringently can perhaps be seen most clearly in the case of military conscription. The Court has permitted conscientious objection to military service on religious grounds, despite the fact that the defense of the country would surely be considered among the most important government objectives. The Court has also been quite flexible in defining religion for the purpose of draft exemption and has allowed private personal codes to serve as the functional equivalent of religious belief. See *U.S. v. Seeger* (1965) and *Welsh v. U.S.* (1970). For a more detailed analysis of religious issues related to conscientious objection, see Pfeffer 1983; 1984.

10. During the 1993 term, the Court overturned a Hialeah, Florida, ordinance that banned religious animal sacrifice *(Church of the Lukumi Babalu Aye v. City of Hialeah)*. Some observers have argued that this decision represents a return to the libertarian understanding of the free-exercise clause that characterized earlier Court decisions. In our view, such an interpretation is incorrect. The Hialeah ordinance specifically identified religious sacrifice as the proscribed practice, a prohibition that seemed to be aimed at the Santeria religion. Were Hialeah to pass a general ordinance against animal slaughter within its borders, it might be unlikely (given Scalia's opinion in *Smith*) that the Santerians would be allowed an exemption based on their presumed rights to exercise their religion freely (see Kilpatrick 1993). Mary Bendyna, however, has argued that the *Smith* decision was an anomaly, and that the general logic of the case is unlikely to be repeated (personal communication, 1993).

11. This is part of a wider pattern of increasing constitutional litigation in many areas.

12. The precise extent to which the Court can control its own agenda is a matter of some controversy. For a more expansive view of the Court's discretion in this area, see Perry (1991).

13. To illustrate how gradually this process has occurred, consider the case of the exclusionary rule, which holds that evidence in a criminal trial that has been gathered illegally may not be used against a criminal defendant. The exclusionary rule was applied to the federal government in 1914 *(Weeks v. U.S.)* but was not applied to state governments until 1961 *(Mapp v. Ohio)*.

14. For similar classifications of possible positions on church–state relations, see Casanova 1994, 56; and Robbins 1993.

2

Religion and Politics:
A Contested Public Space

A recent mailing from the Christian Coalition contained the following appeal:

> The radical left [has a] strategy to *silence* Christian voices and *suppress the Christian vote for the critically important 1994 Congressional Elections. . . . They want to intimidate Christians into staying out of the political process. . . .* The liberal majority which controls Congress *desperately wants to shut down and silence Christian and pro-family broadcasters.* (emphasis in original)

The specific piece of legislation to which this mailing represents a response was a measure termed the "Fairness in Broadcasting Act."

A recent "Special Memorandum and Report" from the American Civil Liberties Union (ACLU) to its members dealt with "attacks on religious liberty and separation of church and state." The mailing read, in part:

> Christian extremists are orchestrating a massive, nationwide *defiance* of the Bill of Rights and Supreme Court rulings . . . the most extensive, heavily funded effort *ever* by the Religious Right to force religious indoctrination into our public schools. . . . The political arms of the Religious Right are taking over school boards, which the ACLU will have to sue when they *inevitably impose their Christian extremist agendas. . . .* [The Religious Right] *exhibits the kind of narrow thinking that will eventually foment the religious strife that has torn apart other societies. . . .* (emphasis in original)

The threat that this mailing attributes to the Religious Right is the possibility that prayers might be read at high-school graduation ceremonies if "requested" by a majority vote of graduating seniors.

Increasingly, the rhetoric of interest groups who are attentive to religious issues contains the sort of hyperbolic statements contained in the above passages. The strong emotion exhibited in both mailings illustrates that conflict over the relationship between church and state in the United States is frequent and often intense. The reasons for such conflict are not difficult to discern. The United States exhibits more religious diversity than most other nations and has an unusually high level of religiosity (Wald 1992; Kosmin and Lachman 1993). When citizens differ widely in their religious beliefs and identities, and care passionately about them, religion will frequently become the subject of political dispute. Religious issues are unlikely to be pushed off the political agenda for reasons of indifference or consensus. Disputes over matters considered important by large numbers of people are the "stuff" of political conflict.

Although the issue of church–state relations has enlivened American politics for approximately a half century, few empirical studies have investigated systematically public attitudes toward the roles of religion in political discourse. We hope that the data on which this book is based, and our analyses of these data, will fill an important gap in our understanding of public opinion on the meaning of the religion clauses of the First Amendment.

Our purpose in this chapter is to provide an overview of the data sources used in this book and to profile the most basic attitudes of Americans toward issues of religion and politics. How religious are Americans? How religiously diverse are the American people? How do Americans react to religious issues in American politics or to citizens falling outside their particular religious traditions?

The Data

The data for this study came from three sources. First, we relied on two telephone surveys conducted for the Williamsburg Charter in December 1987. A national sample of 1,889 adult Americans aged eighteen and over and a quota sample of elites were selected, and respondents were asked a series of questions on church–state issues.[1] Households were selected through random-digit dialing, and respondents within the household were selected according to a set of rules to assure a representative distribution on age and gender (see Hunter 1990 for details).

Seven samples of elites were surveyed. University faculty in Ph.D.-granting departments of political science, sociology, history, and English were surveyed, yielding 155 respondents. Business leaders were sampled from *Who's Who in Business and Finance,* producing 202 respondents. Government leaders were also sampled: 106 respondents were selected from a sample of the top 3,000 career and political appointees in federal government departments and agencies. A sample of nationwide radio and TV news directors who were members of the Radio and Television News Directors Association, along with newspaper editors in cities of more than 100,000 as listed in *Working Press of the Nation,* produced 100 respondents. Three separate sets of religious leaders were selected from diocesan offices,[2] churches, and synagogues: 101 Protestant ministers, 100 Catholic priests, and 99 Jewish rabbis were included in the sample. The aggregation of these groups does not constitute a random sample of American elites but rather a purposive sampling of groups from various sectors of society.[3]

The survey instruments included two questions on abstract positions on religious establishment and a series of concrete questions on religious establishment and free exercise. Many of the concrete questions focused on issues that have been addressed by the U.S. Supreme Court, including public displays of Christianity, the use of public monies for religious purposes, the teaching of religion in schools, the regulation of religious traditions commonly referred to as "cults," and the role of non-Judeo-Christian religions in America. Additional questions focused on the relationship between religion and democracy and the proper role of religious leaders in political activity.

The surveys are the richest available source of national data on public opinion on church–state issues, but they suffer from several problems. Nearly all of the questions in the survey are dichotomous—that is, they ask respondents to choose between two alternatives with no options provided for intermediate responses. Moreover, there are no filters to separate out those respondents who have not thought about a question or who may have no real opinion.

The survey instrument therefore creates measurement error. First, those who have no real attitudes on a particular issue may respond to a question randomly. Although respondents were allowed to indicate that they had no opinion on an issue and many did so, research has shown that many respondents feel social pressure to try to answer survey questions. They may feel a desire to please or impress the interviewer, or they may be embarrassed to show their lack of knowledge. This may lead them to randomly respond or to respond to subtle cues in the wording of questions.[4] This problem is frequently referred to as the problem of "nonattitudes" (for an extended review, see Asher 1992). The best way to deal with this potential problem is to design a survey that invites those with no opinion to abstain from answering a question. This was not done with the Williamsburg Charter surveys, and we will therefore use special statistical and analytic techniques to partially ameliorate the problem.

The problem of nonattitudes is greatest on topics on which the public has little information. There are reasons to believe that many Americans may have poorly formed attitudes on some of the concrete church–state issues that will be the focus of later chapters. Many Americans have little information on the structure and functioning of government, and this applies to the constitutional principles of the First Amendment. In the Williamsburg mass survey, only a third of respondents knew that freedom of religion was guaranteed in the First Amendment.[5]

On the other hand, the pervasive effects of religious affiliations, beliefs, and behaviors on political attitudes (Leege and Kellstedt 1993) suggest that religious elites may provide the mass public with some relatively straightforward cues on political issues, including those that involve church–state relations, and that the public may therefore have meaningful opinions on these issues even in the face of little concrete information. Even though a Baptist may not have thought much about abstract issues of church–state relations, for example, she may have heard sermons at her church or by televangelists that argue that America is a Christian nation or that the separation of church and state is important. A Catholic who has given little thought to the meaning of the term "establishment" may have had interfaith encounters with Jews and use those experiences to mold his opinions on whether city officials should be permitted to display the menorah. He also may have gone to a Catholic school and therefore may have strong opinions about some aspects of government support for religious education. Thus the public may not need much concrete information about the structure of the Constitution or the history of case law to have relatively coherent positions on many church–state matters.

A second problem with dichotomous questions in the Williamsburg survey is that they force individuals to choose an absolute category when they may have a strongly held but subtle and nuanced position. Imagine, for example, that we measure support for public displays of the nativity scene on city property on a 1-to-5 scale, where 1 indicates complete opposition to such a display and 5 indicates strong support. Some individuals may take a position similar to that of the U.S. Supreme Court—that a nativity display is appropriate as part of a larger set of cultural symbols relevant to the Christmas holiday but that such a display involves the establishment of religion if it stands alone. On this 1-to-5 scale, these individuals may score 4. Yet in response to a dichotomous question, they must either entirely support or entirely oppose the nativity display. Again, this problem is best dealt with at the stage of survey design by avoiding dichotomous items.

A final problem with the data lies not in the wording of the questions but in their ordering in the survey. Research has shown that the ordering of questions may influence the responses of citizens, in part by priming them to consider certain issues (see Benton and Daly 1991; Schuman and Presser 1981; Sigelman 1981; McFarland 1981; and Schuman, Presser, and Ludwig 1981). For example, at one point in the Williamsburg survey, respondents were asked whether they support displays of nativity scenes on city property. The very next question asked if the respondent approves of displays of Jewish candles on city property. There are doubtlessly a number of Americans who would favor a crèche on city property but oppose a display of Jewish candles, but by asking the questions consecutively, the survey forces these individuals to publicly confront the apparent inconsistency in their attitudes and therefore produces more support for the menorah than would otherwise appear.

Similarly, respondents were asked if they supported government-funded chaplains for the military, and those that answered in the affirmative were then asked if they supported Buddhist chaplains. It seems likely that at least some people first supported funding military chaplains that they assumed to be Christian then indicated support for funding for Buddhist chaplains in order to seem fair and consistent. If the question on funding Buddhist chaplains had been asked immediately after a question on Satan worship, fewer people would have indicated support because in that hypothetical ordering the respondent would have been primed to consider the dangers that some non-Judeo-Christian religions might pose.[6]

The problem of question ordering therefore makes our measurement of the establishment of a non-Christian faith imprecise. It creates an additional problem as well—one of correlated measurement error. The error in measurement in support for Buddhist chaplains and for public displays of Jewish candles is correlated to the answers to the questions on Christian chaplains and public displays of the nativity scene. Only those who favored spending on Christian chaplains or who favored public displays of the nativity scene would be affected by the question ordering, and those affected would always choose a particular response—in favor of allowing displays of the menorah and in favor of funding Buddhist chaplains. Thus the error in measuring the "true" attitudes toward funding Buddhist chaplains or displaying the menorah is correlated with the position on the questions on Christian chaplains or displays of the nativity.[7]

Despite these problems, the data from the Williamsburg surveys are clearly worth examining. First, the surveys are the most comprehensive national surveys of public opinion on church–state matters ever conducted. Second, there is evidence that a majority of the public responded to these questions in meaningful ways. There is a surprisingly high level of consistency in the public response across many issue areas. Moreover, a fairly sizable portion of the public took positions on some issues but indicated that they had no opinion on others, suggesting that most respondents did not feel inordinate pressure to appear to have an opinion on all issues but, rather, were willing to admit that they had not thought about certain issues and lacked the information to form an opinion.

The measurement problems described above may be at least partly alleviated through the creation of attitude scales that combine several specific questions and by the use of sophisticated statistical techniques such as latent structure analysis (LISREL) that allow the modeling of response error. LISREL is a statistical technique that allows researchers to account for the effects of measurement error in relationships between variables. Throughout the analyses in this book, we have estimated most equations in LISREL and in more accessible techniques such as OLS regression. Although the book seldom presents the results of the LISREL analyses, they always confirmed the basic results presented here. In general, the LISREL analysis suggests that although there is substantial measurement error in the data, the public does hold meaningful, consistent opinions on church–state matters (Wilcox 1993).

The Williamsburg surveys included a rich variety of items that measure concrete attitudes on establishment questions, but they contained far fewer questions to measure support for free exercise of religion. To supplement the data from the Williamsburg studies, we conducted our own telephone survey of residents of the Washington, D.C., area. Interviewing took place in November of 1993 and yielded more than 600 usable questionnaires.[8] The response rate was a very respectable 74 percent. The survey instrument included most of the establishment questions from the Williamsburg Charter survey, along with a number of items tapping abstract principles and specific applications of the free-exercise clause.

Methodologically, the Washington area survey has some advantages as well. Most of our questions were cast in the form of five-point Likert scales (ranging from strongly agree to strongly disagree), which allowed respondents to select intermediate responses and made it easier to indicate "no opinion" when that response was appropriate. This should minimize the problem of nonattitudes. We also varied the question ordering from the Williamsburg Charter surveys to avoid the problem of correlated measurement error.

We were also able to include a variety of items that measure important religious orientations, such as religious self-identifications and charismatic religious experiences (see Wilcox 1992 for discussions of these types of items). Thus, in several important respects, we hope our use of the Washington area data supplements gaps in the Williamsburg Charter studies.

Of course, those who live in Washington, D.C., and its suburbs differ in many ways from Americans in other areas. Compared to the national public, Washington area residents are far better educated, more affluent, and more politically informed. Washington, D.C., and its Maryland suburbs contain a sizable number of middle-class blacks, and Washington also contains many less affluent and less well-educated African Americans as well. Finally, the Washington area has become a multicultural metropolis, with immigrants from most countries living and working in close proximity to one another.

However, these data have certain advantages as well. The racial, ethnic, and especially religious diversity of the area mean that residents can be expected to have relatively frequent interaction with people from outside their particular religious tradition. Many Washington, D.C., area residents may have given more thought to some free-exercise questions for interactions with individuals of non-Christian faiths are more common. The fact that the survey was conducted in and near the nation's capital suggests that church–state issues might be unusually visible and perhaps unusually salient as well. This possibility may well mitigate the nonattitude problem discussed above.

Finally, in order to get some understanding of the meaning behind the patterns in these data, we have conducted in-depth interviews and focus groups with respondents from various religious traditions. The subjects were not randomly selected, and the interviews were discursive in nature. These more qualitative data were gathered in the areas surrounding the District of Columbia and Chicago. Of course, the individuals who participated in these interviews and focus groups are not a random sample of all Americans. Insights from these interviews should be interpreted as suggesting possible explanations for the patterns of the survey response, not as representing solid social scientific evidence for a particular interpretation. These qualitative studies are intended to illustrate patterns found in the more systematic samples of the Williamsburg and Washington surveys.

Thus, this book is based on three distinct sources of public opinion data. Each source brings some unique strengths and weaknesses to our exploration into public attitudes toward church–state relations in the United States, and we are hopeful that, taken together, they provide a reasonable comprehensive picture of an important issue in contemporary American politics.

Religiosity in the Mass Public and Elites

The abstract and concrete issues of religious separation and free exercise that are discussed in the following chapters are complex, and reasonable legal scholars and religious figures disagree on most of them. Most American do not have the time to ponder such questions nor the interest to motivate them to examine carefully their ramifications. In the absence of a carefully reasoned position, respondents will likely rely on their past socialization, both in their schools and churches.

Those citizens who have studied social sciences in colleges and universities have been exposed to some of the issues involved in church–state issues, and in general that socialization has probably supported religious separation and the free exercise of religion by minorities. A variety of studies have shown that formal education is a strong predictor of support for civil liberties and especially for the protection of the rights of minorities (see Stouffer 1955; Nunn, Crockett, and Williams 1978; Prothro and Grigg 1960; McClosky and Brill 1983; Wilcox and Jelen 1990; but see also Sullivan, Pierson, and Marcus 1982). Yet education is not the only, or perhaps even the most important, source of attitudes on church–state issues.

During the past two decades, research on religion and politics has established that religious affiliations, doctrine, and involvement are all important predictors of political attitudes. We now know that individual churches instill specific political beliefs in their members (Wald, Owen, and Hill 1988; 1990; Jelen 1991a). Pastors may attempt to socialize their members into specific positions on political issues (Jelen 1994) or support political organizations or candidates with positions on church–state issues (Guth 1984; 1989), congregants may serve important political discussion partners (Gilbert 1993), and organizations that span the interstitial zone between religion and politics may recruit their members from among the active members of churches (Himmelstein 1986). In addition, Americans may get political cues from their exposure to televangelists (Jelen and Wilcox 1993; Wilcox 1988; Welch and Leege 1991).

Of course, religious socialization on political issues is likely to be highest on issues that deal directly with religious matters. The response of many pastors to the Court decisions in the 1960s banning school prayer was intense and immediate. Many local pastors and priests decried these decisions and predicted dire consequences to the spiritual life of the nation. More recently, televangelists such as Jerry Falwell and Marion (Pat) Robertson have frequently centered their televised sermons or discussions on issues of church–state relations. Religious elites take positions on church–state issues and communicate them to their followers. This would suggest that religion will be a major source of attitudes on these types of issues.

Table 2.1 shows the religious affiliations, behaviors, and beliefs of the general public in the Williamsburg Charter data and the Washington, D.C., sample. A large majority of Americans indicated some sort of affiliation with a religious tradition. Of course, some of those who call themselves Catholics or Protestants or Jews have not entered a church in many years except for weddings or funerals. Yet this general willingness to express a psychological affiliation with a religious tradi-

Table 2.1

Religion and Religiosity among the Mass Public
(percentage of each sample falling into each category)

	Williamsburg	Washington
Mainline Protestant	25	19
Evangelical Protestant	33	16
Nontraditional Protestant	*	2
Catholic	28	36
Christian, No Specific Denomination	*	9
Jew	2	3
Non-Judeo-Christian	*	4
No Preference	13	12
Religion Very Important in Life	51	*
Religion Not Important in Life	10	*
Attend Church Weekly	42	23
Never Attend Church	11	17
Bible Literally True	31	13
Born Again	27	17
Liberal Christian	*	41
Fundamentalist Christian	*	9
Evangelical Christian	*	15
Charismatic or Pentecostal Christian	*	11
Charismatic Experience	*	10

Notes: Non-traditional Protestants in the Washington area sample include Mormons, Christian Scientists, and other groups.
  *Question not asked.

tion is far more common in the United States than in Europe (Wilcox 1988).

We have divided those who identified themselves as Protestants into mainline Protestants and evangelicals.[9] In recent years, the cultural divide between mainline Protestants and their evangelical counterparts has become more visible. Mainline Protestant churches include Episcopalian, Presbyterian, Methodist, and some Lutherans, and these churches have been associated with relatively accommodating responses to secularization and modernity (Hunter 1983; 1987; Jelen 1993a). Their leadership has also been associated with liberal political activism. Pastors from mainline Protestant denominations led protest marches against segregation in the 1960s and against the war in Vietnam in the 1960s and 1970s. A number of mainline churches have debated or endorsed fairly liberal cultural positions on such issues as women's rights, abortion, and sexual morality (Jelen 1993a).

In contrast, evangelical denominations, including Southern Baptists, independent Baptist and fundamentalist churches, the Assembly of God and other pentecostal denominations, and various holiness churches have maintained conservative positions on cultural issues and have become increasingly active in politics (Wilcox 1992; Wald 1992). Evangelical churches differ from mainline Protestant denominations by their emphasis on the authority of the Scriptures. Evangelicals believe that the Bible contains no errors, and some take the stronger position that every passage is literally true. Most evangelicals also emphasize the importance of a personal religious conversion experience that is commonly referred to as being "born again" although not all evangelicals use that language to describe their experiences (Kellstedt 1989).

Evangelical churches once were somewhat detached from politics and preached the importance of keeping separate from the secular, sinful political world. In 1976, Jimmy Carter, a born-again Southern Baptist who regularly taught Sunday School, urged evangelicals to become involved in politics and brought many previously apolitical evangelicals into the electorate (Wilcox 1992). In 1978, Christian Right organizations such as the Moral Majority and Christian Voice followed suit, urging evangelicals to vote against Carter in favor of Ronald Reagan, a political conservative who seldom attended church services but who took positions on religious and social issues that appealed to Christian Right leaders. This political activity by prominent evangelical leaders led many of the rank-and-file to become involved in political action, but others remained deeply skeptical of involvement in secular politics (Wilcox, Linzey, and Jelen 1991).

Evangelicals are not a unified group; there are deep divisions between fundamentalist evangelicals, pentecostal evangelicals, and other, more moderate evangelicals (Wilcox 1992; Jelen 1994; Beatty and Walter 1988; Smidt 1988; 1989). Fundamentalists (such as Jerry Falwell) believe that the Bible is literally true and that it is the ultimate source of any knowledge of God's will (see Falwell 1980). In contrast, pentecostals, charismatics (such as Pat Robertson), and some holiness Christians stress the importance of the revelations of the Holy Spirit, often during ecstatic religious experiences. Many pentecostals and charismatics practice glossolalia (speaking in tongues), faith healing, and being "slain in the Spirit." Finally, moderate evangelicals (such as Billy Graham) maintain that the Bible is the inerrant but not necessarily literal word of God and do not engage in the ecstatic religious experiences of the pentecostals. These divisions may have prevented a unified Christian Right movement in the 1980s (Wilcox 1992). Yet all three groups are part of the broad evangelical Protestant tradition in the United States. In this book, evangelical churches will generally be considered together although in a few cases fundamentalists and/or pentecostals take different positions from more moderate evangelicals, and these differences will be noted.[10]

Roman Catholics have been increasingly assimilated into American life over the past few decades although many of the Catholics in these data readily identified their ethnic roots. The Catholic church has claimed the authority to take strong positions on moral and political issues and even occasionally to expel church members who do not agree. This position has been most evident on abortion although the National Conference of Catholic Bishops have taken positions on a variety of other issues such as income distribution and nuclear weapons.[11] This religious socialization has had some mixed results: Catholics do hold different positions from non-Catholics on issues ranging from abortion to foreign policy (Cook, Jelen, and Wilcox 1992; Jelen 1994), but the differences are fairly small. Moreover, many American Catholics are unwilling to accept as authoritative the pronouncements of Catholic elites (see especially McNamara 1992).

Although Catholics may agree with Protestants on many issues of religious establishment, it seems likely that there will be certain issues that involve religious doctrine on which Catholics will be more likely to oppose establishment. In particular, Catholics are likely to object to establishment of specific doctrines or prayers because they are likely to involve Protestant theology. Garry Wills argued that "Catholics withdrew from the public school system to escape Protestantism, not secularism. Prayers were still said, the Bible still read, in schools that the Catholic hierarchy objected to—only it was the Protestant translation of the Bible that was used, and the Protestant version of the Lord's Prayer" (1990). This suggests that we might expect Protestant–Catholic differences to be largest on establishment issues that involve specific religious prayers or that involve religion in the classroom.

Catholics remain a religious minority in America, and at various points they have been the target of hostility by some members of the Protestant majority. Organized anti-Catholic activity was common in the latter part of the nineteenth and the first half of the twentieth century (Lipset and Raab 1978). This history may have produced stronger support among Catholics for free exercise of religion because they may be able to empathize with the problems facing other religious minorities.

American Jews are an even smaller minority, one that has been persecuted for centuries in Europe and elsewhere. Many Americans who identify themselves as Jews are claiming a cultural, not a religious identification. Indeed, fully 60 percent of Jews in the General Social Surveys between 1972 and 1991 reported little attachment to organized religion while only 10 percent reported behaviors and attitudes that evidence high levels of religiosity (Cook, Jelen, and Wilcox 1992). Yet the cultural identification alone may be enough to mold attitudes toward church–state issues. Most American Jews may support church–state separation, regardless of their level of religiosity. Most instances of public displays of religion involve Christian symbols, and although the *Lee v. Weisman* case involved a rabbi offering a prayer at high school graduation, some Jews see such public displays of Judaism as opening the door to still further displays of Christianity. Indeed, the Weisman family who objected to the rabbi's prayer were Jews who had previously objected to a Christian prayer at their elder daughter's graduation. Jews may favor church–state separation for other reasons as well. Some object to the display of the menorah on public land because it distorts the Jewish faith by emphasizing a minor celebration that coincides with Christmas, mixing the Jewish celebration with the larger Christian and secular holiday.

Yet Jews are likely to be especially supportive of free exercise of religion, especially for non-Christian religions. As with Catholics, Jews may identify with the isolation and persecution of religious minorities. One Jewish college professor told us that "when they take away the right to practice Shinto or Buddhism or Native-American religions, they are one step away from limiting my right to practice my religion."

Table 2.1 includes not only a listing of the religious affiliations of respondents to the Williamsburg Charter survey and the Washington, D.C., study, but it also shows their religious doctrine and their level of religious involvement. In the Williamsburg data, two items measured religious doctrine: One asked whether the Bible was literally true, and the second asked whether the respondent had been "born again." When using the Williamsburg Charter data, those who believed that the Bible is literally true and who reported a born-again experience were coded as evangelicals.[12] Not all of those who attend evangelical churches hold evangelical religious beliefs, and some of those who attend mainline Protestant and even Catholic churches hold these beliefs, suggesting the need to distinguish between denomination and doctrine.[13] In the Washington, D.C., data, the Bible item allowed respondents to distinguish between a literal interpretation of the Bible and one that held that the Bible was inerrant. In Table 2.1 we show the percentage who held that the Bible is literally true to allow comparison with the national survey data, but when using the Washington area data we defined evangelicals more appropriately as those who believe in the inerrancy of Scripture and who report a born-again experience. Finally, two items in both surveys measured religiosity: One asked the importance of religion in the respondent's life, and one asked frequency of church attendance.

The Washington area survey contained some of the same religious variables as the Williamsburg survey, with some additional religious items as well. In addition to denominational preference and church attendance, the Washington study contained questions concerning religious self-identification and an item measuring religious experience. However, the Washington survey did not contain an item measuring the importance the respondent attaches to religion. The precise question wordings are shown in the appendix.

Table 2.1 shows that a quarter of the Williamsburg sample claimed an affiliation with a mainline Protestant church, and a third identified with evangelical denominations, suggesting that the sample slightly overrepresented evangelicals. Twenty-eight percent of respondents were Catholics, 2 percent were Jews, and 13 percent had no religious affiliation. Approximately half claimed that religion is very important in their life, while only one in ten said religion is not important. More than 40 percent attended church weekly, while 10 percent never attended religious services. Approximately a third indicated the Bible is literally true, while a quarter reported a born-again experience.

The Washington area survey showed some similarities and differences with the Williamsburg data. Washington residents were about half as likely as the national sample to report an affiliation with an evangelical denomination, and they were slightly more Catholic. Nearly 10 percent of Washington, D.C., residents identified themselves as merely "Christian," and 4 percent reported affiliations outside the Judeo-Christian tradition, such as Buddhist, Muslim, Taoist, or Hindu. Our Washington, D.C., area survey contained no more Jews than the national sample (although our Washington sample contained a higher percentage of Jews) and no more respondents who claimed no religious affiliation. However, respondents in the Washington sample were less religiously observant and less doctrinally orthodox than members of the Williamsburg sample. Washington area residents were much less likely than respondents to the Williamsburg study to believe in a literal Bible and were more than half as likely to report having been born again. In terms of religious self-identification, nearly half the Washington sample reported identification as liberal Christian, while approximately one in ten identified as a fundamentalist, evangelical, or charismatic or pentecostal Christian.[14]

The data from the elite sample in Table 2.2 provide an interesting contrast to the data from the mass samples in Table 2.1. The most secular group was academics, where nearly half of the sample claimed no religious affiliation and indicated that religion is not important to their lives, and fully a third never attend church. The media, business, and government elites were also more secular than the general public although a substantial minority of each group attended church weekly and indicated that religion is very important in their lives. Indeed, there were far more highly religious members of these groups than members with no religious involvement, suggesting that reports of a lack of religion among elite groups (especially the media) are exaggerated. Far fewer of the members of each of these elite groups held evangelical doctrine or identified with an evangelical denomination than the general public, while mainline Protestants (especially higher-status denominations), those with no religious preference, and Jews were somewhat overrepresented.

The elites who were not religious professionals differed from the general public in their lower levels of religious involvement, their more frequent affiliation with higher-prestige mainline Protestant churches, and their lower levels of religious orthodoxy. In addition, they were better educated.[15] All of this would suggest that they would be more supportive of separationist positions on church–state issues and more tolerant of non-Christian religions and therefore more supportive of a broad reading of the free-exercise clause.

Not surprisingly, the three groups of religious leaders showed high

Table 2.2

Religion and Religiosity among Elites
(percentage of each group falling into each category)

	Academics	Business	Government	Media
Mainline Protestant	30	42	44	41
Evangelical Protestant	1	13	15	9
Catholic	14	27	22	25
Jew	9	7	5	7
No Preference	45	12	14	19
Religion Very Important in Life	11	49	43	31
Religion Not Important in Life	46	12	23	19
Attend Church Weekly	12	32	36	34
Never Attend Church	33	9	12	17
Bible Literally True	1	11	12	11
Born Again	3	18	14	16
	Ministers	Priests	Rabbis	
Mainline Protestant	46	—	—	
Evangelical Protestant	54	—	—	
Catholic	—	100	—	
Reformed Jewish	—	—	28	
Conservative Jewish	—	—	44	
Orthodox Jewish	—	—	27	
No Preference	—	—	—	
Religion Very Important in Life	100	98	93	
Religion Not Important in Life	—	—	2	
Attend Church Weekly	100	99	96	
Never Attend Church	—	—	—	
Bible Literally True	60	—	—	
Born Again	81	36	—	
Pope Infallible?		59		
Observe Kosher			73	

levels of subjective and public religiosity. A substantial percentage of Protestant ministers believed that the Bible is literally true (even among the mainline churches) and reported a born-again experience. More than a third of Catholic priests reported a born-again experience while fewer than six in ten believed the Pope is infallible. Among Jewish rabbis there was representation of the three main theological traditions—reformed, conservative, and orthodox. These religious elites were more deeply involved in religious activity than the general public and, therefore, might be more likely to support public displays of religious faith. Yet they were also generally better educated, suggesting that they might be more supportive of free expression by religious minorities.

Taken together, the data in Tables 2.1 and 2.2 suggest a mass public and an elite stratum that are divided on the basic tenets of religion and religious belief. Many elite groups (with the obvious exception of the clergy) were less orthodox and less religious than members of the mass public although religion and religiosity were well represented within virtually all elite groups. Perhaps more telling, the data in these tables show substantial variation *within* groups of elites as well. With the sole exception of the virtual invisibility of evangelical affiliations and beliefs within academia, the myth of a uniformly secular elite stratum receives little support here. Thus, to the extent that mass publics respond to elite cues, elite dissensus on religious matters seems likely to exacerbate the religious diversity of the American public.

Mass and Elite Views of Religion and American Democracy

Before examining public and elite attitudes toward issues of church–state relations, it is useful to get an overview of attitudes on related matters. How important is religion to the American political system? Do Americans believe that religious people are civil participants in public discourse, or does the zeal of their faith render them too intolerant to compromise? Do they view some religious groups as threats to democracy, and if so, what do they believe should be done about them? Tables 2.3 and 2.4 present data from the Williamsburg surveys that show the attitudes of the general public and of elites on the role of religion in American politics.

Consider first attitudes on the importance that the president have some sort of religious faith. Scholars have argued that the president is a key figure in the civil religion of the United States and that the president has certain "priestly" functions for which a religious faith is a prerequisite. Kenneth Wald argued that "the presidency seems to play a crucial role in American civil religion" (1992, 60). Mark Roelofs suggested that the president plays a prophetic role in "congregating the people as a covenanted presence in history" (1992, 1). Ronald

Table 2.3

Mass Attitudes on Religion and Society
(percentage of each group falling into each category)

	Mass
Very Important for President to Have Religion	33
Somewhat Important for President to Have Religion	37
Would Vote for:	
Minister	77
Catholic	91
Born-Again Baptist	87
Jewish	89
Greek Orthodox	85
Atheist	33
Religion Is Essential for Democracy	16
Religion Is Helpful but Not Essential	32
Religion in Politics Will Divide Society	32
Religious Tolerance Has Declined	53
Religious People Are Intolerant	62
Religious Politicians Are Hypocrites	43
Freedom of Religion Is in Constitution	71
Of those with an opinion:	83
Freedom of Religion Is in First Amendment	33
Of those with an opinion and who knew religion is in Constitution:	75
The ACLU Files Too Many Religious Lawsuits	67
Have Heard of "Secular Humanism"	28
Think Schools are Teaching "Secular Humanism"	12
Of those who have heard of it:	60
Media Is Unfair to Some Religious Groups	49
Supreme Court Should Decide Separation of Church and State	75
Some Religious Groups Are a Threat to Democracy	51
Of those:	
Evangelical/Religious Right	12
Atheists/Secular	6
Nazi/Klan/Racist Right	23
Non-Christian Religions/Cults	22
Should Restrict Public Acts by These Groups	19
Of those who named a group:	53
Some Religious Groups Have Too Much Influence	34
Of those:	
Catholics	38
Jews	12
Evangelicals/Religious Right	48
Atheists/Secular	2
Non-Christian Religions/Cults	8

Table 2.4

Elite Attitudes on Religion and Society
(percentage of each group falling into each category)

	Academics	Business	Government	Media
Very Important for President to Have Religion	6	24	18	15
Somewhat Important for President to Have Religion	14	37	39	34
Religion Is Essential for Democracy	3	15	11	4
Religion Is Helpful but Not Essential for Democracy	14	29	22	39
Religion in Politics Will Divide Society	38	16	21	13
Religious Tolerance Has Declined	18	19	22	31
Religious People Are Intolerant	65	55	54	55
Religious Politicians Are Hypocrites	44	34	32	41
Freedom of Religion Is in Constitution	72	71	64	78
Of those with an opinion:	76	82	70	84
Freedom of Religion Is in First Amendment	54	49	33	55
Of those with an opinion and who knew religion is in Constitution:	84	77	75	86
The ACLU Files Too Many Religious Lawsuits	15	56	40	41
Have Heard of "Secular Humanism"	92	56	80	76
Think Schools are Teaching "Secular Humanism"	39	26	25	26
Of those who have heard of it:	44	57	38	40
Media Is Unfair to Some Religious Groups	20	39	38	25
Supreme Court Should Decide Separation of Church and State	88	82	79	77
Some Religious Groups Are a Threat to Democracy	57	54	54	45
Of those:				
Evangelical/Religious Right	75	35	29	30
Atheists/Secular	0	0	0	0
Nazi/Klan/Racist Right	36	17	25	36
Non-Christian Religions/Cults	19	18	25	7
Should Restrict the Public Acts by These Groups	7	14	14	8
Of those who named a group:	16	38	33	24

(continued)

Table 2.4 *(continued)*

	Academics	Business	Government	Media
Some Religious Groups Have Too Much Influence	28	22	28	24
Of those:				
Catholics	40	38	27	43
Jews	13	17	26	9
Evangelicals/Religious Right	90	52	50	52
Atheists/Secular	0	0	0	4
Non-Christian Religions/Cults	3	2	12	4

	Ministers	Priests	Rabbis
Very Important for President to Have Religion	58	51	14
Somewhat Important for President to Have Religion	37	37	45
Religion Is Essential for Democracy	40	25	6
Religion Is Helpful but Not Essential for Democracy	42	50	34
Religion in Politics Will Divide Society	20	8	33
Religious Tolerance Has Declined	47	26	13
Religious People Are Intolerant	57	28	46
Religious Politicians Are Hypocrites	28	12	31
Freedom of Religion Is in Constitution	78	83	81
Of those with an opinion:	80	87	84
Freedom of Religion Is in First Amendment	50	67	63
Of those with an opinion and who knew religion is in Constitution:	79	90	88
The ACLU Files Too Many Religious Lawsuits	67	75	36
Have Heard of "Secular Humanism"	73	92	86
Think Schools are Teaching "Secular Humanism"	51	69	30
Of those who have heard of it:	73	80	39
Media Is Unfair to Some Religious Groups	67	66	46
Supreme Court Should Decide Separation of Church and State	71	72	91
Some Religious Groups Are a Threat to Democracy	61	56	78
Of those:			
Evangelical/Religious Right	26	23	51

(continued)

Table 2.4 *(continued)*

	Academics	Business	Government	Media
Atheists/Secular	13	4	1	
Nazi/Klan/Racist Right	35	24	43	
Non-Christian Religions/Cults	22	18	10	
Should Restrict the Public Acts by These Groups	27	22	21	
Of those who named a group:	53	46	30	
Some Religious Groups Have Too Much Influence	35	12	35	
Of those:				
Catholics	9	0	0	
Jews	0	0	0	
Evangelicals/Religious Right	50	33	63	
Atheists/Secular	9	0	0	
Non-Christian Religions/Cults	27	0	12	

Wimberly measured support for civil religion in part by agreement that "we should respect a president's authority since his authority is from God" (1976). This symbolic presidential role in our civil religion may be useful in building legitimacy, for Smidt found that children with high levels of civil religion were more supportive of political authority (1980; 1982).

This would suggest that many Americans need to be reassured that a presidential candidate has a religious commitment before they can support him because without religion it would be difficult for him to carry out his "priestly" role. Clearly many of our presidents have used civil religion in their rhetoric (Hart 1977; Toolin 1983). Reagan used religious language regularly, and this practice apparently was sufficient to overcome his lack of religious observance in gaining the support of Christian Right leaders and activists. Bill Clinton's use of religious language in his 1992 presidential bid was probably partially responsible for the Democratic ticket's increased share of the white evangelical vote.[16] Indeed, Clinton's use of the phrase "new covenant" in his acceptance speech to the Democratic National Convention in July of 1992 made explicit use of biblical imagery.

The data in Table 2.3 show that a substantial majority of the American public believe it is important our president has religious beliefs. In Table 2.4, majorities of business and government elites and large majorities of religious elites also agreed on the importance of a president having religious convictions although a narrow majority of media elite and a large majority of academics thought religion is unimportant for a president.

The responses to this general question are borne out in a series of specific items asking whether the respondent would be willing to vote for a candidate with various religious ties. These items were asked of the general public but not of the various elite groups. Large majorities of the general public showed a willingness to vote for candidates from a variety of Judeo-Christian traditions, and a somewhat smaller majority seemed willing to vote for a minister, but only a minority were willing to vote for an atheist. These data suggest that Americans see a need for their president to have religion, though it need not be their personal religious faith. This finding in turn suggests that most Americans are not very particularistic in their reported levels of presidential support. Presidential religion is obviously approached at a very general level by a clear majority of the U.S. population.

It is somewhat surprising that such large majorities indicated a willingness to vote for candidates from such a variety of religious traditions. It is likely that at least some of these respondents were making what is obviously the socially acceptable response of religious tolerance but that once in a voting booth they would hesitate to support a candidate from a religious tradition greatly different from their own. Because these questions were asked consecutively, any unwillingness to support a candidate of a different religious faith would be immediately obvious to the interviewer, and some respondents might have avoided such a display of religious prejudice.

Yet many Americans did indicate an unwillingness to vote for candidates of different faiths. Although this table does not show differences across religious traditions, evangelical Christians were notably less willing to vote for a Catholic, a Jewish candidate, or a Greek Orthodox than were other Americans, while the small number of Jews in the survey were less likely than other respondents to indicate a willingness to vote for a born-again Baptist. Overall, however, majorities of those in each religious tradition indicated a willingness to support a candidate from a different church and an unwillingness to vote for an atheist.

This finding suggests that Americans regard the appropriate political use of religion as consensual. It seems plausible to assert that such Americans who desire a religious president but are indifferent to the particular faith may want the president to be concerned with spiritual and ethical matters, regardless of the particular religious views he or she may hold. As one focus group respondent said: "The end of all religions is the same: to get in touch with yourself, and get in touch with a higher being. . . . It doesn't matter if a person is Buddhist, Catholic, Jewish, whatever."

Although Americans want their president at least to profess a religion, they are divided on whether religion is important for democracy. Less than half of the mass sample indicated that religion was helpful to democracy, and a sizable minority responded that religion in politics would divide society, that religious politicians are hypocrites, and that religious people are intolerant.[17] The public is clearly fearful of the potential for religious fervor to divide, and worried that deeply religious people may take extreme and unyielding positions. Indeed, the substantially smaller portion of the public who indicated a willingness to vote for a minister for president may point to a view that religion is a good thing only in moderation.

Among the elite samples, a large majority of Protestant ministers and Catholic priests believed that religion is essential or helpful for democracy, but among all other groups only a minority took that position. Majorities of all elite groups except priests and rabbis believed that religious people are intolerant, and sizable minorities of each group except priests agreed that religious politicians are hypocrites.

These results suggest a certain ambivalence on the role of religion in American political life. Although a majority of Americans wish to maintain the civil religious tradition of the president as religious symbol, many fear that religious passions will prove divisive to the country. Although this survey was conducted in 1987, the 1992 Republican National Convention was the sort of event that increases these fears. Patrick Buchanan's call for a "religious war," coupled with speeches by Pat Robertson and Jerry Falwell, appears to have alienated many Americans. One Republican pollster told one of us that his focus groups after the convention showed that many deeply religious Americans feared the intolerance that they perceived in these speeches and that terms such as "conservative" were increasingly associated with the Religious Right by many participants.

As we noted in chapter 1, most issues of church and state are settled by the Supreme Court, and one of the most frequent litigants in these matters is the ACLU. A majority of the general public believed that the

ACLU files too many religious lawsuits, but they also believed that the Supreme Court should be the source of the ultimate decisions on questions of church–state separation. Among elites, support for the Court as arbitrator of church–state issues was very high, and a majority of academics, government officials, media gatekeepers, and rabbis disagreed that the ACLU is too active in courtroom activity to enforce separation.[18]

The public and elites were divided on whether the media is unfair to certain religious groups, and there was even greater division about exactly which groups are unfairly treated. Indeed, there was such a scattering of groups listed in response to these questions that none were selected by a sizable percentage of respondents. Half of the mass sample believed that at least one religious group is a threat to democracy. Because the questionnaire provided for multiple responses, it should be noted that some respondents selected more than one group as representing such a threat. Of those who perceived a threat to democracy from a religious group, half supported restricting the public actions of that group.

Many respondents reported a belief that certain religious groups have disproportionate influence on American politics. Among those who believed that at least one group was too powerful, the Religious Right was selected by nearly half the mass sample, while over a third of the respondents believed that Catholics wield unacceptable influence. Despite scholarly and media attention to anti-Semitic groups that believe in Jewish or Zionist conspiracies, only about one respondent in ten regarded Jews as too powerful, and such beliefs about atheists and non-Christian religions were even rarer. Again, because the survey instrument permitted multiple responses on these issues, it is inappropriate to add these percentages together.

Nevertheless, the data in Tables 2.3 and 2.4 suggest that, at both the mass and elite levels, there is considerable belief that some religious groups lie outside the acceptable bounds of American politics and pose genuine threats to the American political system. Even among elites who could normally be expected to respect the principles of the First Amendment (academics and media elites), there was measurable (albeit limited) support for restricting the activities of members of such religious groups.

In Table 2.5, divisions between mainline and evangelical Protestant ministers are shown. These two groups agreed on the importance of religion in America, but evangelical ministers were consistently more

Table 2.5

Mainline and Evangelical Differences: Protestant Ministers

	Mainline	Evangelical
Somewhat Important for President to Have Religion	38	37
Religion Is Essential for Democracy	35	44
Religion Is Helpful but Not Essential for Democracy	49	40
Religion in Politics Will Divide Society	15	27
Religious Tolerance Has Declined	45	53
Religious People Are Intolerant	51	61
Religious Politicians Are Hypocrites	20	35*
Freedom of Religion Is in Constitution	76	78
Of those with an opinion:	77	79
Freedom of Religion Is in First Amendment	49	52
Of those with an opinion and who knew religion is in Constitution:	83	75
The ACLU Files Too Many Religious Lawsuits	54	74*
Have Heard of "Secular Humanism"	90	64*
Think Schools are Teaching "Secular Humanism"	50	53
Of those who have heard of it:	60	87*
Media Is Unfair to Some Religious Groups	56	80*
Supreme Court Should Decide Separation of Church and State	72	69
Some Religious Groups Are a Threat to Democracy	58	65
Of those:		
Evangelical/Religious Right	48	10*
Atheists/Secular	5	25
Nazi/Klan/Racist Right	38	27
Non-Christian Religions/Cults	24	20
Should Restrict the Public Acts by These Groups	17	36*
Of those who named a group:	37	67*
Some Religious Groups Have Too Much Influence	28	40*
Of those:		
Catholics	1	18*
Jews	0	8
Evangelicals/Religious Right	90	12
Atheists/Secular	6	12
Non-Christian Religions/Cults	5	41
N	43	51

*$p < .05$.

likely to think that religion and politics make a divisive mixture, that religious people are intolerant and that religious tolerance has declined, and that religious politicians are hypocrites. Although the number of evangelical ministers was too small to be certain, it appears that there were two groups of evangelical pastors in the sample: those who enthusiastically endorsed political activity by religious leaders and those who emphatically disapproved (for similar results see Langenbach 1989; Langenbach and Green 1992).

Evangelical pastors were more negative toward groups and ideas identified by the Christian Right for attack: the ACLU, the media, and the teaching of secular humanism. Mainline ministers were far more likely to see the Religious Right as a threat to democracy while evangelical ministers were more likely to want to restrict the activities of some religious groups and to think that Catholics have too much influence in society.

Finally, these tables provide one indicator of the level of information of mass and elites on church–state issues. A majority of the mass public correctly indicated that freedom of religion is in the Constitution although smaller numbers appeared to know that the religion clauses are located in the First Amendment. It is important to remember that these dichotomous questions give a 50 percent chance of guessing the correct answer, and that in both cases the question is worded in such a way as to elicit positive guesses, which are the correct answers (see appendix). This suggests that the true level of public information is probably lower. Somewhat surprisingly, elites were not noticeably more able to locate freedom of religion in the Constitution and the First Amendment than was the general public.

Conclusions

This chapter has introduced three data sources upon which we will draw throughout the book and which taken together provide a useful portrait of public opinion on church–state issues. Although the public has probably not thought carefully about most of the issues in this book, it seems likely that they will have reasonably coherent attitudes, primarily because of the role of religion in shaping opinion. Religion is salient to members of the American mass public, and religious leaders often provide clear cues to their followers on these issues. Substantively, the data presented in this chapter demonstrate that the attention paid to issues of church–state relations by the legal system is to a large extent motivated by the attitudes of the general public. Political religion remains a persistent problem in American politics for at least three reasons. First, religion is quite salient to most Americans. To relegate religious discourse to the sideline of the public arena is to dismiss as politically irrelevant a large portion of the central concerns of the American people. The strong importance of religious values to many Americans suggests that proponents of various religious perspectives will continue to make claims on the American political system.

Second, American religion is quite diverse. The data presented in this chapter suggest that although some aspects of religion are important to large groups of Americans, there is no consensus on denominational affiliation or religious doctrine in the United States. The fact of great diversity at the elite level further suggests that members of the mass public may receive inconsistent cues from political, economic, and religious elites concerning desirable or acceptable religious attitudes.

Finally, this religious diversity is a source of concern for many Americans. Large minorities of Americans regard some religiously motivated perspectives as unfit participants in American public life. Despite apparent constitutional guarantees of religious neutrality (something to which even most legal accommodationists would assent), many Americans regard members of some groups as threatening, and base that judgment on the content of the group's beliefs. Moreover, our data also suggest that many have a more general fear of the potential for religiously divisive conflict.

Thus, our data suggest that many U.S. citizens have a moth-and-flame perspective on church–state relations. Simply put, religion is an important part of American politics because religious values are important to many Americans. Conversely, the entry of religion into the public sphere, when combined with the sheer diversity of religious belief in the United States, creates certain risks that worry many Americans.

Notes

1. The Williamsburg Charter study included a separate oversample of young people, which we do not analyze in this study.
2. The fact that the Catholic priests were all diocesan priests may skew the sample somewhat. Approximately one-third of all priests belonged to religious orders and were not assigned to diocesan offices. The diocesan priests presumably had lower levels of education than those in religious orders and may have differed in their attitudes on church–state matters as well.
3. Thus, the data derived from the elite samples are not probability samples of

any population, and the analyses of these surveys should be treated with caution. In particular, it is quite problematic to generalize to all American elites from the aggregation of these subsamples.

4. For example, respondents with no real attitude on church–state issues may respond based on whether the question mentions laws, whether the question uses words like "forbid" or "allow." See Payne 1980.

5. More than twice that number knew that freedom of religion was mentioned *somewhere* in the Constitution. However, the general lack of awareness of the location of that right suggests a low level of information about church–state constitutional issues and about the Constitution more generally.

6. Hunter (1990) has cited that a majority of Americans supported funding Buddhist chaplains as evidence of American tolerance of religious diversity. Yet the question ordering was obviously purposive. Immediately after the question on Buddhist chaplains, respondents were asked if they wanted to change their response to the more general item on chaplains. Only seven respondents, or less than one-half of 1 percent, did. It should be noted that the question on Buddhist chaplains was asked only of those who indicated support for funding of military chaplains in general. For the purposes of this book, those who opposed the funding of military chaplains are coded as having opposed the funding of Buddhist chaplains. It is possible that a few Buddhist respondents might have favored such a policy but opposed funding of chaplains in general. A careful inspection of the responses to the survey suggests that this would involve, at most, one respondent.

7. To test the impact of question ordering, we administered variants of the Washington, D.C., survey (discussed below) to several classes of first-year undergraduate students at Georgetown University, varying the question ordering and instructions in each case. The results suggest that although question ordering did indeed matter, the effect was relatively small. Compared to the Williamsburg Charter ordering, approximately 5 percent fewer students favored displays of the menorah when the question was asked much earlier in the survey than the question on the nativity scene. The drop in approval of Buddhist chaplains was 10 percent.

8. The survey was conducted through the auspices of the Department of Government at Georgetown University, using student interviewers who were trained and monitored. There was little racial bias in response rates, perhaps in part because of the popularity of the Georgetown basketball program, but there was an educational bias (meaning that telephone surveys tend to overrepresent people with higher levels of education), as there is in most phone surveys. The data have been weighted by education.

9. Evangelical denominations included most Baptists, the Assembly of God and other pentecostal denominations, the Church of God and various holiness churches, the Missouri Synod Lutheran, some reformed churches, and several other small denominations. The list of evangelical denominations was adapted from one provided by Lyman Kellstedt.

10. The decision to generally treat evangelicals as a single group rather than distinguishing among the different theological communities was made on both practical and empirical grounds. There were simply too few respondents to divide evangelicals too finely, and the data suggest that on most of these issues the various evangelical theological subgroups resembled each other in their attitudes.

11. When Guam was considering a restrictive abortion law that it passed in the aftermath of the *Webster* decision, the bishop threatened to excommunicate any Catholic legislator who voted against the bill.

12. In fact, many evangelicals would reject the position that the Bible is literally true, arguing instead that the Bible is merely inerrant. Yet there is evidence that when nonliteralist evangelicals were confronted with a choice between declaring the Bible literally true or not, they chose the literal option as the closest to their true position. See Jelen (1989).

13. Some analysts have excluded Catholics from possible classification as evangelicals by fiat, but these data suggest that a minority of Catholics hold evangelical doctrinal beliefs. Indeed, more than a third of the priests in Table 2.2 reported a born-again experience. For a greater discussion of Catholic evangelicals, see Jelen (1994); Welch and Leege (1991); and Wilcox (1992). Because a born-again experience is not part of traditional Catholic teachings or theology, more research is needed to understand fully the nature and meaning of this result. Catholic priests and the Catholic laity only rarely indicate a belief in a literal Bible.

14. Of course, respondents were allowed multiple identifications, and there was some overlap between the three "conservative" self-identifications.

15. In the Williamsburg Charter surveys, the education level of elites was not assessed. It seems likely that most media gatekeepers and government elites have at least a college education and that religious elites and academics have advanced degrees. The education levels of business leaders may be somewhat lower although most are likely to have attended at least some college.

16. Exit polls showed that George Bush won 55 percent of the white evangelical vote, a substantial decrease from the approximately 80 percent in 1988. Yet as a group, evangelicals were among the most loyal in the Republican coalition: Recall that Bush received only 38 percent of the general election vote. Still, evangelicals shifted their votes more frequently than non-evangelicals. In 1988, Bush received about 26 percent more votes from evangelicals than from other Americans, and in 1992 the gap was reduced to 17 percent.

17. Interestingly, this response was highest among liberal mainline Christians, Jews, and those with no religious ties and also among evangelical Protestants who hold evangelical doctrine and are strongly involved in religion. Many of these latter respondents may have been echoing what one fundamentalist minister in the Moral Majority told one of us in Ohio in 1983: "I am *not* tolerant of other views because there is only one true view and that is in the Bible. There is no reason for any other view to be heard."

18. Among the secular elite groups, only business leaders believed that the ACLU files too many suits, and this may be due to their general aversion to lawsuits.

3

Abstract Views of Church–State Relations

It has often been noted that the U.S. Constitution is not a document containing detailed policies but is rather a general framework within which American politics is conducted. The Constitution contains the rules under which political conflict is managed and the most general values underlying the practice of political competition. As we noted in chapter 1, the brief, spare language of the religion clauses of the First Amendment has occasioned the contemporary controversy over the meaning of religious establishment and free exercise of religion.

When the justices of the U.S. Supreme Court evaluate the types of issues discussed in chapter 1, they generally use abstract general principles to justify their votes. Many political activists and scholars who take positions on concrete issues of religious establishment or expression attempt to link these positions to some underlying philosophic position. A substantial amount of discourse among scholars and among political and religious elites concerns these abstract principles of church–state issues.

Although political elites may reason from abstract principles to concrete applications (or at least attempt to justify their positions with reference to these principles), it is not clear how many Americans have ever considered the abstract questions of religious establishment. More than three decades ago, Philip Converse (1964) wrote that few Americans understood abstract political terms such as "liberal" and "conservative" and that the public was largely incapable of reasoning from abstract principles to concrete positions.

Converse's classic study used data from surveys conducted nearly forty years ago. Many scholars have argued that the American public today is more sophisticated than the public of the 1950s depicted by Converse (for an excellent summary of this extensive literature, see Asher 1992). The public is better educated today than it was in 1956 and 1960, politics is perhaps more ideological, and ideological labels are more frequently bandied about.

Yet in 1984, the public was not entirely certain which of these terms to apply to Ronald Reagan. Although Reagan had been the most conservative U.S. president in some time and had been in office for nearly four years, only 45 percent correctly identified him as either "conservative" or "strongly conservative" in a national survey before the election. Fully one in five identified Reagan as a liberal, and another 20 percent were unable to use ideological labels. After the election campaign in which Reagan consistently used the label "conservative" and painted Mondale as a "liberal," 60 percent correctly placed him as a conservative, but again 20 percent called Reagan a liberal.[1] This suggests that one in five Americans guessed incorrectly about Reagan's ideology. If a similar percentage guessed correctly, this would mean that only four in ten Americans *knew* that Reagan was a conservative after four years in office and a campaign that emphasized ideological labels.

It may be, however, that the public's grasp of terms such as "liberal" and "conservative" is not a good indicator of its ability to formulate and use abstract principles on issues such as church–state matters. Terms such as "liberal" and "conservative" are frequently used by politicians in misleading ways, and the public might be forgiven for its confusion on the meaning of a term like "liberal" when that label was used by Richard Nixon to describe George McGovern, by George Bush to describe Michael Dukakis and Bill Clinton, and by some conservative Republicans to describe George Bush. Moreover, elites frequently argue about what position a "true conservative" or "true liberal" should take on deficit reduction, taxes, and abortion.

Some political scientists have suggested that the public is capable of organizing their political attitudes around fairly general abstract principles. For example, Jon Hurwitz and Mark Peffley (1987) reported that such abstract principles on foreign policy are important in structuring the foreign-policy cognitions of the general public. They argued that affect toward and beliefs about the Soviet Union were generally accessible principles that allowed most people to make sense of the world.

This and other studies jointly suggest that the public not only has abstract political values and orientations but also that these abstract principles help guide individuals in forming concrete positions on political issues.

So it is possible that the public may hold some meaningful abstract positions on church–state matters. This would not mean that the public has a sophisticated grasp of the nuances that pervade case law on religious establishment issues or that the public uses these abstract principles to determine their stands on specific issues. But it is possible that these values are associated with, and might even help shape, views on concrete church–state issues.

The Williamsburg Charter surveys contained two general questions on religious establishment. The first asked respondents whether government should support all religions equally or not support any religion. The second asked whether the government should take special steps to protect the country's Judeo-Christian heritage or whether there should be a high wall of separation between church and state. Both were dichotomous, forced-choice items.[2]

Most respondents to the Williamsburg survey were able to offer an opinion on whether the government should help religion, but one in six respondents were unable to respond to the "high-wall" question. Of those with an opinion, 46 percent favored offering no help to religion, and 62 percent favored a high wall of separation. Of course, because these questions are dichotomous, this means that just over half of all respondents who offered an opinion wanted to help all religions equally, while just over a third wanted to help protect our Judeo-Christian heritage.

Although the question on a high wall of separation or government protecting a Judeo-Christian heritage appears fairly straightforward, the item on aid to religion is more complex. Those who favor helping all religions equally may take a nonpreferentialist position, believing that government must be neutral among religious traditions but that it need not be neutral between religion and irreligion. This, of course, is the classic accommodationist position and goes directly to the heart of the accommodationist/separationist debate.

For some, this neutrality may only apply to Christian denominations: In chapter 1 we labeled these citizens as Christian preferentialists. Others may support aid to the Jewish or even non-Judeo-Christian faiths—a group we called religious nonpreferentialists. Given the consensual nature of accommodationism, it would be surprising if some respondents did not desire to exclude non-Christian (or non-Judeo-Christian) religions from government's "benevolent neutrality." If one of the political purposes of religion is to provide a basis for social integration and political authority, there would obviously be clear limits as to the types of religion deserving of governmental assistance.

Those who believe that the government should not help religion, however, may take this position for a variety of reasons. Some may believe that the government should not help all religions but only the one true faith—their church. Others may feel that less government is always better and that the government has no business expanding its sphere of influence by aiding religion. Many of these proponents of limited government may interpret this question to center on government *financial* aid to religion. Alternatively, those who oppose government aid to religion may believe that the government should not help religion because such help would come with strings attached. For example, some independent Baptists do not want state aid for their private religious schools because it might entail state regulation of the qualifications of teachers and the content of the curriculum. As one evangelical respondent told us: "I'm strongly opposed to religious schools taking federal subsidies. If we take the government money, we might become accountable to government in questions [of curriculum]. We might also become dependent, lose the ability to be self-supporting."[3]

Some respondents may also be quite skeptical of the ability (or willingness) of government to attain genuine equality among religions. As one person told us: "Different denominations teach different things. At some point, either the notion of 'religion' becomes so vague that anything would count or government would have to make choices about *which* religious values to support. If that happened, our denomination is so small and controversial, we'd be left out."

These two abstract questions each have two options, yielding four possible combinations of positions.[4] Slightly over a third took consistently separationist positions, favoring maintaining a high wall of separation and not helping any religion. Approximately a third took consistently accommodationist positions favoring protecting our Judeo-Christian heritage and helping all religions equally.

As we noted in chapter 1, however, accommodationists and separationists differ in the variety of religious traditions to which they would extend free-exercise claims, and they doubtlessly differ in the nature of religious groups that they believe the government should or should not help. It is possible to infer some of the meaning from these abstract positions by examining positions on concrete issues. Some accommodationists favor helping all religions, including those outside of the Judeo-Christian tradition. Fully 61 percent favored funding Buddhist chaplains, and nearly a third opposed restrictions on Hare Krishna solicitations at airports.[5]

However, many accommodationists probably favor helping all Christian religions, or perhaps helping Christians and Jews but not helping those from religions outside of the Judeo-Christian tradition such as Muslims, Buddhists, Bahaists, Shintoists, or Taoists. Two-thirds wanted restrictions on the free exercise of religions such as Hare Krishna, and nearly one in five thought there is no room in America for Muslims. If these respondents did not want such non-Judeo-Christian religions to worship freely in America, it is highly unlikely that they would support government aid to these religious groups.

Not all respondents took consistently accommodationist or free-exercise positions. Some took positions that favor accommodation on one question and support a separationist stand on the other. These positions may initially seem contradictory, but it is possible that some who hold these positions have relatively sophisticated rationales for them.

More than one in five supported helping all religions equally but also supported a high wall of separation between church and state instead of protecting a Judeo-Christian heritage. It is difficult to construct a thoughtful rationale for this position, but it is possible that a few of these respondents favored a true position of government neutrality on religion—supporting all religions, including those outside the Judeo-Christian heritage. Their support for a high wall of separation may be in fact their rejection of an official endorsement of the Judeo-Christian religious tradition. Thus, at least some of these respondents may be religious nonpreferentialists. Nearly a third of all respondents who favored helping religion but opposed protecting our nation's Judeo-Christian heritage were generally supportive of aid to and protection of such religious groups as Buddhists, Hare Krishnas, and Muslims.[6] For these respondents, a high wall of separation may be preferable to government establishment of Christianity. Government should help all religions and be neutral among them.

Yet it is likely that many of those in this category had not thought much about church–state issues and were responding to the phrasing of the questions. Helping all religions equally sounds fair and impartial, and respondents with no real opinion on the topic were likely to select that option. The high wall of separation of church and state may resonate with memories of high-school civics classes and therefore also provoke a positive response. In short, at least some of the people in this category were probably expressing nonattitudes, selecting what seemed to be the most socially acceptable answer.[7]

Finally, approximately one in ten respondents wanted to protect America's Judeo-Christian heritage but not to help all religions equally. Some of these respondents may want to establish Christianity in general and therefore reject aid to, say, Muslims; others may want to establish a particular type of Christianity. Thus fundamentalist Baptists may not want to help Catholic schools but nonetheless may want to establish the nation's Judeo-Christian heritage. These respondents would fit our category of Christian preferentialists.

Others who hold this set of positions may want symbolic endorsements of religion (public prayers, religious phrases on our money) but do not want the United States to provide *financial* help to religions. For example, one focus-group member responded to a question on religious holiday displays on public property as follows: "Oh, that doesn't bother me. . . . People have needs to celebrate their faith. . . . There's no problem with taxes since there's very little money involved." This group of "symbolic accommodationists" seek only government endorsement of religion, not direct financial aid.

The Washington area study also contained three items relating to attitudes toward church–state relations at a relatively high level of abstraction. As noted in chapter 2, each item was posed in the form of a Likert scale (strongly agree, agree, neither, disagree, strongly disagree):

> The government should not provide help to religion.
> We should maintain a high wall of separation between church and state.
> The government should protect our Judeo-Christian heritage.

Despite some substantial differences in question wording from the Williamsburg surveys, we were able to produce the same basic categories of abstract positions on church–state issues. Although there were some differences in the frequency of response patterns (which we believe to be attributable to differences between the Washington population and the country as a whole), our ability to discern similar patterns in the two datasets makes us confident that we are, in fact, measuring similar phenomena.[8]

Social-Group Differences in Abstract Views

Much political activity in America is centered on the political behavior of social groups. Presidential candidates appeal for the Catholic and/or evangelical vote, the black and/or Hispanic vote, the youth vote, and the Southern vote. Such appeals can work because members of different social and demographic groups frequently hold similar opinions on political issues, and group appeals based on policy promises may succeed if most or even many group members favor those policies.

Some social-group differences in political attitudes are the result of social processes. If college graduates hold different attitudes than those who failed to finish high school, we generally assume that the process of acquiring additional education inculcates certain attitudes into students. If those who frequently attend Catholic religious services differ in their attitudes from nominal Catholics who seldom attend, we assume that the exposure to homily messages or the interaction with congregants influences attitudes.

We must always be cautious in these interpretations, of course, because we are usually not directly observing the process itself but instead drawing inferences from the responses to a survey. It may be, for example, that those who choose to frequently attend Catholic services hold different attitudes from those who do not attend services, so the relationship we observe is not due to social interaction at all but, rather, to the decisions made by individuals with different attitudes about whether to attend religious services.

We also explain social-group differences in attitudes by referring to other factors on which the groups vary. For example, racial differences in attitudes may be due to a number of other demographic differences between blacks and whites: Whites on average have higher levels of education and income; blacks are more likely to attend religious services, to live in the South, and to be young. To determine if these other factors cause group differences, we *control* for these other factors. Intuitively, we compare blacks and whites who have equal levels of education and income, who attend church at the same frequency, who live in the same region, and who are the same age. If the blacks and whites who are similar on these other variables hold identical attitudes, then we conclude that race is not a source of attitudinal differences. If racial differences remain even when we compare similar sets of black and white respondents, then we must look further to explain racial differences in attitudes. In practice, we do not actually search for such similar respondents from different races to a national survey but instead use statistical procedures to perform the same basic function.

Religious Differences

It should come as no surprise that religious affiliation, doctrine, involvement, and salience are all associated with abstract attitudes toward religious establishment. The effects of these religious characteristics differ somewhat across the two abstract questions, and there are subtle patterns of interactions among them.

Before examining actual differences in attitudes among those who belong to various religious traditions, it is useful to consider what differences we might expect based on the histories and doctrines of the churches discussed in chapter 2. It seems likely that mainline and evangelical Protestants will differ in their attitudes on religious establishment. Mainline Protestants are likely to embrace a separationist position on establishment issues for many mainline churches have strongly supported separation of church and state. The official position of these churches may be communicated through occasional sermons and study documents, and the attitude of the laity may be influenced by these communications.

Evangelicals are likely to be more supportive of protecting our nation's Christian heritage. Evangelical religious leaders have frequently endorsed the idea that America is a Christian nation, and some have pointedly refused to even qualify that statement to note the *Judeo*-Christian heritage. Yet many evangelicals are likely to oppose helping all religions for a variety of reasons.

First, many evangelical churches (especially Baptists) have a long tradition of support for church–state separation. Second, some may oppose support for all religions because that would entail support for religions that are not part of the "true" faith. Fundamentalist evangelicals have frequently been associated with religious intolerance, including a dislike of Catholics (see Wilcox 1992; Reichley 1985; and

Bradley 1987).[9] Fundamentalists and some other evangelicals may oppose helping all religions equally because that would possibly entail providing aid to Catholic schools. Some Christian Right leaders have gone further and argued that a "neutrality" between religions has led to the teaching of witchcraft in schools. One candidate for the school board in San Diego in 1992 told his supporters that the military services have official witches, presumably as part of a truly non-preferentialist policy of selecting military chaplains.

Roman Catholics and Jews have long been religious minorities in Protestant America, and anti-Catholicism and anti-Semitism was once widespread (Lipset and Raab 1978). It seems likely that Catholics and Jews will be somewhat supportive of a high wall of separation between church and state for religious minorities may especially appreciate protection from imposition of the dominant religious traditions. Yet Catholics in particular may also favor helping all religions equally. Catholic schools have frequently sought public funds for various programs, and at least some individual Catholics are likely to interpret questions on aid to religion as involving financial support for Catholic schools.

Table 3.1 shows the abstract establishment positions of members of different religious denominations. Consistently separationist attitudes —support for a high wall of separation and no aid to religion—were most common among mainline Protestants and respondents with no religious preference. Catholics and members of evangelical denominations were most likely to be pure accommodationists—favoring aid to all religions and protection of a Judeo-Christian heritage. Although many Jews took a purely separationist position, a plurality favored a high wall of separation but government aid to all religions. Apparently, many Jews favored helping all religions equally but were skeptical of preserving the nation's Judeo-Christian heritage, despite the apparent inclusion of Judaism within the protected tradition. It is of some interest that Catholics—another religious minority—did not appear to share such skepticism. Although relatively few respondents wanted to protect a Judeo-Christian heritage with no aid to religion, evangelical Christians were disproportionately likely to hold this position.

Table 3.1 also shows the relationship between religious doctrine, salience, and church attendance on abstract establishment attitudes. Respondents who held evangelical *beliefs* (an inerrant Bible and a born-again experience) were more likely to be either pure accommodationists or to favor protection of a Judeo-Christian heritage without

Table 3.1

Social Characteristics and Abstract Views of Establishment
(percentage of each group falling into each category)

	High Wall/ No Help	High Wall/ Help All	Protect/ No Help	Protect/ Help All
Religious Group				
Mainline Protestant	42	22	11	26
Evangelical Protestant	26	20	13	41
Catholic	30	22	8	39
Jewish	37	42	0	20
No Preference	54	19	4	23
Religious Doctrine				
Evangelical	27	11	17	45
Non-evangelical	38	23	8	31
Religious Salience				
Very Important	28	19	14	39
Somewhat	39	25	6	30
Not Important	63	17	4	16
Church Attendance				
Every Week	31	17	15	38
1–2 Times/Month	27	27	7	39
Few Times/Year	42	24	6	28
Never	55	21	2	22
Sex				
Men	43	21	11	26
Women	30	22	9	40
Race				
White	40	20	10	31
Black	15	31	5	49
Hispanic	20	28	9	42
Age Cohort				
Pre–World War II	42	16	11	30
World War II	40	21	11	29
Sixties/Seventies	36	21	9	35
Reagan Era	27	27	7	39
Region				
Northeast	35	24	6	35
Midwest	35	18	11	36
South	35	23	9	34
West	40	20	12	28

(continued)

Table 3.1 (continued)

	High Wall/ No Help	High Wall/ Help All	Protect/ No Help	Protect/ Help All
Education				
Less than High School	25	24	8	42
High School	26	25	9	40
Some College	38	21	9	32
College Graduate +	51	16	12	22
Income				
Lowest Quarter	25	23	7	45
Middle Half	39	23	9	30
Highest Quarter	44	18	12	26
Ideology				
Liberal	41	24	6	29
Moderate	35	24	7	34
Conservative	35	18	15	32
Partisanship				
Democrat	35	27	6	32
Independent	39	21	7	34
Republican	37	17	14	32

Source: Williamsburg Charter Survey.

aiding all religions equally. Evangelical doctrine appeared to have its greatest effect on support for preserving the nation's religious heritage. Non-evangelicals were most likely to hold separationist beliefs but were also twice as likely as theologically orthodox evangelicals to support separation but equal aid to all religious groups, perhaps indicating support for religious nonpreferentialism.

Those whose religious views were very important to them were most likely to be pure accommodationists and to disproportionately favor protection of the Judeo-Christian tradition with no equal aid to religion. Not surprisingly, a large majority of people who believed religion to be unimportant were separationists. When religious salience was measured as church attendance, a slightly different pattern emerged. People who attended church at least once a month were likely to be accommodationists while infrequent attenders were likely to be separationists. Very frequent attenders (at least once a week) were disproportionately likely to favor protection of a Judeo-Christian heritage but to oppose equal aid to religions, perhaps an indication of Christian or even denominational preferentialism.

Demographic Differences

One of the strongest predictors of support for nearly all types of civil liberties is education. Those with higher levels of education are generally more willing to grant freedom of speech and association to unpopular political groups (see Stouffer 1955; Prothro and Grigg 1960; Nunn, Crockett, and Williams 1978; McClosky and Brill 1983; Wilcox and Jelen 1990), more likely to favor legislation that bans discrimination against homosexuals, and more likely to support a woman's right to choose an abortion (Cook, Jelen, and Wilcox 1992). College-educated citizens are most supportive of basic constitutional principles including limited government and separation of powers. It seems likely, therefore, that those with higher levels of education will be more supportive of separation of church and state.

Table 3.1 shows the relationships between education and income and attitudes toward church–state issues. In both cases, the relationships seem straightforward and linear. Those with higher levels of education and income were more likely to support separationism while those with lower levels took accommodationist positions.

Of course, part of the reason that income is related to these attitudes is that income is partly a function of education. Yet when we control for education, family income remains a significant predictor of support for church–state separation. Other analysis suggests that part of this relationship is explained by the higher incomes of two-career families, who are generally less religiously orthodox than families in which the woman chooses to stay home with the children.

In the past decade, political scientists have focused increasingly on gender differences in public attitudes. Most studies have found that women are less supportive of the use of military force in international disputes (Conover 1988; Cook and Wilcox 1991; Wilcox, Allsop, and Ferrara 1993; Bardes 1992; Bendyna and Lake 1994), and other studies have suggested that women are more supportive of spending on social welfare programs and environmental protection (Conover 1988; Shapiro and Mahajan 1986). There is no gender gap in the United States on gender-related issues such as abortion and the Equal Rights Amendment although there are large gender differences on these issues in Europe (Wilcox 1991b). Yet women are also more likely than men to hold orthodox religious views and to worship regularly both in private and in public.

Table 3.1 shows that there were substantial gender differences with respect to attitudes on church–state relations. Women were considerably more likely to take an accommodationist position than men, who were more likely to hold separationist attitudes. The observed gender differences are, in part, attributable to the greater religiosity of American women. However, as will be shown below, gender exerts an independent effect on church–state attitudes, even when the effects of religious variables have been taken into account.

There is also substantial scholarly literature on racial differences in attitudes. African Americans (and to a lesser extent Hispanics) are far more supportive than whites of spending on social programs and on all sorts of government programs to help people and on legislation to protect various groups from discrimination. They are somewhat less supportive of abstract civil liberties positions, primarily because of their lower levels of education. African Americans and Hispanics are more likely to attend church and pray frequently and to indicate that religion is important in their lives. These differences would suggest that whites will be more supportive of church–state separation than either blacks or Hispanics.

Table 3.1 shows racial and gender differences in abstract attitudes toward issues of church–state relations. The survey was administered to more white than black or Hispanic respondents, so the estimates of African-American and Hispanic attitudes are less precise than those for whites. Both African Americans and Hispanics were less likely than whites to hold separationist attitudes and were considerably more likely to be accommodationists. Of particular interest is the relatively high numbers of non-white respondents who wanted to help all religions equally but who opposed government support of a Judeo-Christian heritage.[10]

Public-opinion studies frequently report large differences in attitudes between various generations of Americans. In some cases, these differences are due to individuals' location in their life cycles. As citizens pass through different stages in their lives, their circumstances and needs change. Young single Americans are concerned with obtaining jobs, those who are a few years older are concerned with mortgage rates and child care, those older still are concerned with the quality of schools, and those who are retired are worried about Social Security and Medicare benefits.

Yet some types of attitudes differ among members of discrete generations of citizens. Important events that occur when people are young can mold their views of certain issues throughout their lifetime (Mannheim 1972). There is evidence, for example, that those who reached adulthood during the 1960s are more supportive of feminism (Cook 1993) and of legal abortion (Cook, Jelen, and Wilcox 1992) than those who grew up in earlier or later times.

Table 3.1 shows the attitudes of four age groups: those who reached adulthood before World War II, when many Americans had not traveled beyond the boundaries of their communities and had little interaction with those of different religious traditions; those who came of age during World War II through the late 1950s, when there was greater mobility yet a tremendous concern for social conformity; those who came of age during the 1960s and 1970s, which was a period of great social flux and secularization; and those who reached adulthood during the 1980s, under a conservative Republican president who embraced the support of the evangelical Christian Right and of pro-life Catholics and who frequently endorsed religious establishment.

The data in Table 3.1 show that members of the "Reagan" cohort were least likely to be separationists and most likely to hold accommodationist views. Indeed, they were also most likely to support a high wall with equal aid to religious groups, suggesting that they were very supportive of government aid to religion. This finding may reflect the fact that these people came of age during an administration that took a strongly accommodationist stand on issues of church and state. In general, older respondents were more separationist than younger ones. These data show that cohort differences tend to be monotonic—that is, each cohort is more supportive of separation than the one that is slightly younger.

Finally, with the exception of a slight separationist tendency among Westerners, there appeared to be no important regional differences on church–state attitudes at the abstract level.

Political Differences

In the past two decades, the Republican party has publicly embraced the support of Christian Right leaders such as Jerry Falwell of the now-defunct Moral Majority and Pat Robertson, former presidential candidate and current leader of the Christian Coalition. These figures actively support public displays of Christianity, and the Republican

party national conventions and platform increasingly show the influence of these fundamentalist and charismatic religious leaders. The
visible influence of Christian Right leaders on Republican politics may
lead Republicans to be more supportive of religious accommodation
than Democrats.

However, some research has shown that mainstream Republicans
have reacted with some distaste for the visibility of the Christian Right
within their party (Wilcox 1992) and are quite negative toward Christian Right figures such as Robertson. Indeed, during the early 1990s,
visible battles between Christian Right forces and the old-guard Republicans split party organizations in cities such as Houston and left
bitter feelings in states such as Oregon, Washington, and Virginia
(Rozell and Wilcox forthcoming 1996). This might suggest that partisan differences will not be great. Moreover, Republicans generally are
more likely to oppose government aid to groups and institutions, so
Republicans may be actually less likely to favor aid to religion.

It seems likely that ideology will also be associated with abstract
positions on church–state issues. Conservatives are more likely to support a public endorsement of Christianity, but they may not be unified
behind government aid for religion. For many conservatives, government assistance to any group is problematic, and small government is
always better than a government that takes a positive role in assisting
social groups. Thus we might expect many conservatives to take a
"symbolic establishmentarian" position—wanting to protect our Judeo-
Christian heritage but opposing government aid to religion.

Table 3.1 also shows the relationships between party and ideology
and abstract positions on church–state issues. Liberals were slightly
more likely to be separationists, with moderates the most accommodationist group. Perhaps more interestingly, self-identified conservatives were most likely to favor protection of a Judeo-Christian heritage
but no aid to religion and least likely to take the opposite set of positions. A similar pattern was evident with respect to partisanship. While
there were no differences in party identification among separationists
or accommodationists, Republican identifiers were somewhat more
likely to favor protecting the Judeo-Christian heritage but to oppose
equal aid to all religions and least likely to take the opposite set of
positions. Thus, Republicans and conservatives (many of whom, of
course, are the same people) seemed most likely to desire the preserva-
tion of the nation's Judeo-Christian heritage but to oppose equal aid to

religion. Some were probably symbolic accommodationists who opposed financial aid to religion, and others were probably religious preferentialists who did not want to support religious groups with which they did not agree.

Multivariate Analysis of Social-Group Differences

To gain greater insight into the effects of particular variables on abstract church–state attitudes, we conducted separate multivariate analyses on each abstract item from the Williamsburg survey.* Because both questions are dichotomous, we performed logistic regression analyses on the no help/help all and high wall/preserve Judeo-Christian heritage items. These analyses are presented in Table 3.2.[11]

As these data indicate, there were important similarities and differences in the patterns of variables that predicted responses on each item. Responses to both questions were related to respondent gender, income, age, Roman Catholicism, and religious salience. On both items, women were more accommodationist than men, and this result held up even when the greater religiosity of women was taken into consideration. Similarly, older people were considerably more separationist than their younger counterparts, and, not surprisingly, people who attached greater importance to religion were more supportive of helping religion and of preserving our Judeo-Christian heritage. As noted above, the effects of income on separationism remained significant even when educational attainment had been controlled.

Jews and blacks were more likely than others to support equal assistance to all religious groups. These findings, in combination with the significant effects of Catholicism on this item, suggest that the notion of "helping all equally" was particularly salient to members of religious and racial minorities. Those with greater levels of education were less likely to favor government aid to religion.

By contrast, a different pattern emerged for the equation explaining variation in the "high wall/preserve Judeo-Christian heritage" item. Those who attended church frequently, who perceived that religion is very im-

---

*Multivariate analyses, such as OLS regression and logistic regression, enable us to estimate the unique effects of any given variable when the effects of other variables have been taken into account.

Table 3.2

Multivariate Analysis of Abstract Church–State Items
(logistic regression)

	No Help/ Help All	High Wall/ Preserve Judeo- Christian Heritage
	B	B
Education	−.54***	−.14
Income	−.34***	−.10***
Age	−.02***	−.01***
Sex	.51***	.36***
Black	1.02***	.30
Hispanic	.27	−.20
Southern Resident	.003	−.43**
Ideology	−.08	.20*
Partisanship	−.01	.26**
Evangelical Denomination	.06	.26
Catholic	.54**	.51**
Jew	.95*	−1.63
No Religious Affiliation	.53	.10
Evangelical Doctrine	−.08	.41***
Religious Salience	.23†	.43**
Frequency of Attendance	.02	.21*
Constant	2.82	1.28

Percent Predicted Correctly:			
No Help	60.00	High Wall	82.58
Help All	71.43	Preserve Heritage	44.01
Overall	66.09	Overall	67.98

N	1409	1264

Source: Williamsburg Charter Survey.
†*p* < .10; **p* < .05; ***p* < .01; ****p* < .001.

portant in their lives, and/or who held evangelical religious doctrine were more supportive of preserving the Judeo-Christian heritage.

The data in Table 3.2 also show the importance of political attitudes in explaining responses to the "high-wall" item. Both Republican identifiers and self-described conservatives were likely to endorse special measures to preserve the nation's religious heritage, and this result held up even after the effects of income, education, and religiosity had been taken into account. This result, again, suggests that "Judeo-Christian heritage" is an important symbol of political debate in America. The "separation of church and state" may not only be an important regime symbol but may also be regarded as the arena over which most religious/political issues are contested.

Conclusions

The results presented in this chapter suggest that there is no consensus concerning the political role of religion at the abstract level among the American people. The public is almost evenly divided between those who favor strong separation between church and state in the abstract and those who favor stronger government endorsement of Christianity. Each of these groups constitutes approximately a third of the general public. An additional fifth of all respondents favored government help for all religions but also a high wall of separation between church and state. Most of these respondents were probably choosing the answer they felt was the most socially desirable and were therefore expressing nonattitudes, but some may have been voicing a genuine non-preferentialist position. Finally, a number of citizens wanted to protect our Christian heritage but not to provide aid to all religions. Some of this latter group were preferentialists who wanted to keep government aid from going to support religious traditions that they opposed, while others were symbolic accommodationists, favoring a broad government support of the symbols of Christianity without providing any aid (especially financial aid) to religion.

Although there was substantial overlap, these different positions appeared to attract different constituencies. The notion of equal assistance to religion (a basis of both nonpreferentialism and accommodationism) appeared particularly attractive to religious and other minorities. By contrast, the concept of a Judeo-Christian heritage seemed to connote support for a dominant, majoritarian culture and appeared to be (in the public mind) the subject matter for political conflict in the area of church–state relations.

Although elites are generally thought at least occasionally to reason deductively from abstract positions to concrete applications, most political-science research has suggested that the general public is far less likely to see the connection between its abstract political values and its concrete political positions. The next chapter will examine public attitudes toward concrete issues of church–state establishment.

Notes

1. These data are from the 1984 National Election Study conducted by the Center for Political Studies at the University of Michigan.

2. In our focus-group data, several respondents were uncomfortable with the dichotomies posed by these questions. As one respondent noted with respect to the second item: "Basically, those two categories are too limiting. . . . They're really two separate questions. With the high wall, we're talking about all religions. The other is whether the Judeo-Christian heritage and government should be together. What about government and all religions?"

3. Interestingly, this respondent was quite active in the home-schooling movement and had educated three of her children at home through the primary grades.

4. In fact, there are eight possible combinations if missing data are considered. After careful inspection of the patterns of responses (both of demographic and religious predictors of positions on the abstract questions, and of specific positions on concrete establishment issues), we have coded those who are missing on one question as holding a consistent position in favor of separation or establishment. These respondents differed slightly in their demographic profile from those who genuinely took a consistent position on both issues and were virtually indistinguishable from them in their responses to concrete establishment questions.

5. Of course, this is in fact a free-exercise issue and does not deal directly with establishment.

6. Only two questions dealt with establishment of non-Christian religions— funding for Buddhist chaplains and allowing displays of Jewish candles on city property. More than half of all respondents who took this combination of abstract positions favored both of these policies. But a prerequisite to favoring aid to religions is tolerance of their practice. Approximately a third of respondents who took these two abstract positions favored allowing Hare Krishnas, the followers of the Reverend Moon, and Muslims to practice in America. Approximately one in ten favored free exercise for Satan worshipers and opposed limits on "cults."

7. Of course, this problem occurs in other categories as well.

8. Because respondents could select from five options on each of three questions, there were myriad response patterns. Nearly 70 percent of the Washington, D.C., area respondents fell into the categories mentioned, however.

9. At one Ohio Moral Majority meeting, the Baptist pastor titled his sermon "Roman Catholic Church: Harlot of Rome."

10. We can think of two possible explanations for this pattern. First, blacks and Hispanics may be skeptical of protecting the nation's Judeo-Christian heritage because it elicits a connotation of preserving the dominant American culture, from which non-whites (like Jews) may feel excluded. Alternatively, both groups may be more likely than whites to favor government support of private institutions, including churches.

11. We also performed discriminant analysis of the four categories shown in Table 3.1. The logistic regression results are more easily interpretable.

4

Concrete Views of Church–State Establishment

In the last chapter we showed that the public is generally divided in its abstract positions on religious establishment. There is strong support for a high wall of separation between church and state, but the public is almost evenly divided on whether the government should help all religions equally or not help religions. Of course, people rarely have direct experience with an abstract legal or ethical principle but experience these issues at the level of applications. Moreover, these abstract principles do not always have obvious, direct applications to concrete situations.

Does a high wall of separation between church and state mean that cities cannot display manger scenes at Christmas? What if the display includes secular symbols such as a Santa Claus and reindeer? What if the display includes a menorah for Hanukkah? Does a high wall of separation mean that public prayers cannot be offered at school graduations? What if those prayers are student initiated? What about prayers to begin sessions of Congress? When private religious schools help educate students in a given school district, what level of public assistance is appropriate? Can no tax dollars be used to help students at these schools, or can the state provide some assistance to transport these students or help those with learning disabilities? If prayers are not allowed in the schoolroom, how about a moment of silence? Can student religious groups use school property to hold meetings after school hours? Such questions have vexed political elites as well: When Justice Black first endorsed the high-wall language in *Everson v.*

Board of Education, he voted with the Court majority that a public school district may provide transportation to students to and from private religious schools.

The Supreme Court has ruled on many of the issues noted above, but the justices have divided on each issue, suggesting that the application of these abstract principles to concrete cases is not straightforward. Moreover, we know relatively little about public attitudes on these issues. The available evidence suggests a good deal of support for accommodationist positions on concrete issues such as displays of the nativity scene (Hougland 1992), school prayer (Elifson and Hadaway 1985), and teaching of creationism (Woodrum and Hoban 1992).

This chapter will examine public attitudes on concrete issues of religious establishment. First, it will describe the content of public attitudes—what the public believes about various concrete establishment issues. Next, it will examine how closely these attitudes are related to the abstract positions discussed in chapter 3. Finally, it will explore the sources of concrete attitudes on establishment issues.

Concrete Attitudes on Establishment Issues

The Williamsburg Charter survey included a variety of specific questions on concrete issues of religious establishment, and we included variants on many of those items in our survey of Washington area residents. Some questions asked about matters that have been the subject of litigation, such as government aid to private religious schools, the teaching of evolution, and public displays of the nativity scene and the menorah. Others asked about policies that have rarely been the subject of Supreme Court rulings (Pfeffer 1984), such as funding for military chaplains.

Table 4.1 shows the percentage of respondents who supported separationist and accommodationist positions on a series of concrete establishment issues. The wording of each question can be found in the appendix. Recall that the Washington area survey included a category for undecided or neutral responses, so the percentages are not directly comparable with those of the Williamsburg Charter survey. For the Williamsburg Charter survey, the percentages taking separationist and accommodationist positions summed to 100 percent because those were the only options the questionnaire allowed.

Table 4.1

Public Attitudes on Establishment Issues
(percentage of respondents taking separationist position on each issue)

	Separationist	Accommodationist
Williamsburg Survey		
General Orientations		
No Government Help for Religion	46	54
High Wall of Separation	61	39
Specific Issues		
Prayer in Congress	28	72
Prayer in High School Sports	34	64
Manger Scene on City Land	14	86
Jewish Candles on City Land	16	84
Military Chaplains	7	93
Buddhist Chaplains	34	64
Government Funds for Religious Schools	55	45
Tax Church Property	54	46
School Rooms for Religious Meetings	26	74
Moment of Silence in Schools	20	80
Government Requires Teaching of		
Judeo-Christian Values	63	37
Teaching Evolution Only	88	12
Teaching Evolution and Creationism	76	24
Washington, D.C., Area Survey		
General Orientations		
Government Help for Religion	66	24
High Wall of Separation	74	19
Government Protects Judeo-Christian		
Heritage	37	54
Specific Issues		
Prayer in High School Sports	42	48
Manger Scene on City Land	23	71
Jewish Candles on City Land	31	58
Military Chaplains	15	78
Buddhist Chaplains	29	60
School Rooms for Religious Meetings	30	64
Moment of Silence in Schools	20	64
Government Requires Teaching of		
Judeo-Christian Values	53	36
Teach Evolution Only	41	47

Note: For question wording, see appendix.

For comparison, the percentages who took separationist positions on the abstract questions are included. It is evident from the data in this table that the public is far more supportive of accommodation between church and state on concrete issues than it is in the abstract. Although more than 60 percent of respondents to the Williamsburg survey favored a high wall of separation, large majorities in Table 4.1 favored public prayer, the use of city property to display a Christian manger scene or Jewish candles, allowing student religious groups to use school property, and other establishment positions. This discrepancy was even more evident in the Washington area survey, where nearly three in four respondents favored a high wall of separation between church and state but majorities favored accommodationist positions on most concrete issues.

In both surveys, majorities supported separationist positions on only a few concrete issues. On only three questions in the Williamsburg data did majorities support church–state separation: on teaching creationism alone in the classroom (though a majority favored teaching both evolution and creationism), on taxing church property, and on opposing public funding of religious schools. In the Washington area survey, a small majority opposed mandating that the government require the teaching of Judeo-Christian values in schools.

Two items asked about the use of government funds to support non-Christian religions: whether public displays of the Jewish menorah are appropriate and whether the government should pay for Buddhist chaplains. In the Williamsburg Charter data, these questions were asked immediately after questions on public displays of the crèche and government funding for Christian chaplains. In the Washington area survey, we used a different question ordering, and the results showed a somewhat larger dropoff in support for displays of the menorah.[1] In the Williamsburg Charter data, nearly equal percentages of the public favored displays of a Christian manger scene and Jewish candles, but in the Washington area survey, more than one in eight respondents favored the former but not the latter. This suggests that many of those who answered the Williamsburg survey indicated support for public displays of the menorah in an attempt to appear fair.

The most obvious regularity in Table 4.1 is the high level of abstract support for separation of church and state and the high level of concrete support for religious accommodation. Clearly a substantial portion of the public favors separation in the abstract but accommodation on many concrete issues.

A similar pattern is evident in Table 4.2. The top portion of this table shows the percentage of respondents to the Williamsburg Charter survey who took each of the four general abstract positions who then supported separationist issues on each concrete item. The data in this table show that support for concrete accommodationist positions is high even among those who took separationist positions on both abstract issues. Even among those who thought government should not help religion *and* that we should maintain a high wall of separation between church and state, majorities supported a variety of public displays of Judeo-Christian religion, including prayers in Congress and before high-school sporting events and using city land to display nativity scenes and menorahs. Large majorities also supported a moment of silence in schools and the teaching of both evolution and creationism. Indeed, nearly half of all of those who took abstract separationist positions on *both* items favored accommodation on *each* of four questions about public displays of Judeo-Christian religion—on both questions on public prayer and on both questions on religious symbols.

At the bottom of the table, we present similar information from the Washington area survey. In this part of the table, we compare those respondents who opposed government aid to religion and government protection of a Judeo-Christian heritage, and who also indicated support for a high wall of separation between church and state, with those who took the opposite set of positions. Among these abstract separationists, there is again substantial support for accommodation on concrete issues.

How can those who endorse separation in the abstract consistently support accommodation on concrete issues that apparently involve questions of religious establishment? We will consider two general possibilities in this chapter. First, it is possible that these data are yet another example of inconsistent survey responses by members of the general public who do not carefully consider survey questions and who have poorly formed attitudes on issues that seldom affect their daily lives. As we noted in chapter 3, many political scientists have argued that the public is generally unable to understand abstract political questions or to connect them with concrete issues. This would suggest that few of the respondents understood such terms as "high wall of separation" and that few really thought carefully about whether government should help religion.

Doubtlessly there is some truth to this interpretation. It is likely that

Table 4.2

Concrete Establishment Issues by Abstract Positions

	Separa-tionist	Nonpref-erentialist	Prefer-entialist	Accommo-dationist
Williamsburg Charter Survey (percentage of those who took each combination of abstract positions who took separationist positions on concrete issues)				
Prayer in Congress	40	32	15	17
Prayer in High School Sports	49	35	25	20
Manger Scene on City Land	19	18	5	10
Jewish Candles on City Land	21	20	7	10
Military Chaplains	8	8	6	6
Buddhist Chaplains	16	27	23	30
Government Funds for Religious Schools	75	55	65	30
Tax Church Property	62	54	44	48
School Rooms for Religious Meetings	19	32	18	21
Government Requires Teaching of Judeo-Christian Values	78	72	44	45
Moment of Silence in Schools	32	18	11	10
Teaching Evolution Only	21	8	5	3
Teaching Evolution and Creationism	64	76	75	69
Washington, D.C., Area Survey (percentage of those taking each combination of abstract positions supporting a separationist position on each item)				
Prayer in High School Sports	65		25	
Manger Scene on City Land	36		17	
Jewish Candles on City Land	40		32	
Military Chaplains	22		16	
Buddhist Chaplains	30		33	
School Rooms for Religious Meetings	33		24	
Moment of Silence in Schools	38		6	
Government Requires Teaching of Judeo-Christian Values	84		40	
Teach Evolution Only	56		26	

few of the respondents to this survey had previously given much serious thought to the abstract questions of church–state establishment and that at least some of them would have responded to the questions without considering them carefully. Moreover, at least a few of these concrete issue positions do seem inconsistent with abstract separationist sentiments. For example, it is difficult to construct a rationale for suggesting that government should not help religion but should fund religious schools.

It is also possible, however, that this disjunction indicates something meaningful about the substance of public opinion and that many of the respondents have thoughtful rationales for this set of positions. If we are to argue that the responses represent at least in part meaningful opinion, then we must consider the likely rationales that would lead citizens who favor separation in the abstract to support accommodation at the level of concrete applications. There are several possibilities.

First, some of the concrete issues in the survey involve both establishment and free exercise. The funding of military chaplains may be seen as establishment of religion, but it also may be seen as allowing individuals whose lives are in danger while defending the United States to have access to the religious professionals necessary to exercise freely their faith. The use of school classrooms by student religious groups also involves both establishment and free-exercise issues. When viewed from the standpoint of the establishment clause, the use of public-school facilities for religious purposes appears accommodationist, yet when the same question is considered from the standpoint of free exercise, a prohibition against the religious use of such facilities might be regarded as discriminatory. Recently, the U.S. Supreme Court ruled that religious groups are entitled to use school facilities after hours on the same basis as other groups, and it relied heavily on the free-exercise clause to support its decision (Kilpatrick 1993).

Our focus-group data are interesting on this point. Many respondents did in fact regard many government accommodations to religion as instances of religious free exercise. Government is regarded as an instrument of the popular will, and some respondents argued that excluding religious observance because it involves the use of government is somewhat arbitrary. A young Catholic conservative man argued for the legitimacy of religious holiday displays: "City Hall is public property! Why shouldn't the public be allowed to do what they want with it?" The same respondent reacted to the notion of prayers at high-school sporting events in a similar manner: "Isn't a prohibition on public prayer undemocratic? If a team prays, or a community prays, isn't it their choice?"

Some citizens, then, may have viewed many of the concrete applications as involving the free exercise of religion by individuals and communities. Indeed, some may have seen the abstract issues as not involving church–state separation at all because they might be expected to have the support of most members of the community. That is, a display of a nativity scene is not perceived as an important issue that involves church–state separation because it entails no conflict and is supported by most citizens in the city or county. This result is consistent with other studies: Dick Kaukus (cited in Hougland 1992) reported that only slightly more than a third of Kentucky residents in 1989 believed that a recent controversy over a crèche display was related to the idea of separation of church and state.

Many of our focus-group respondents did not imagine that a particular issue might arouse any controversy and therefore favored accommodation. When the moderator or another group member pointed out that a practice might offend a segment of the community, their immediate response was to back off of their accommodationist position. A middle-aged Jewish woman reacted to the issue of religious holiday display as follows: "If the town wants to do it, and people don't complain, it doesn't bother me. (Suppose someone did complain?) If it becomes an issue, maybe I don't think it should be there at all."

An Episcopalian woman had a similar change of heart. Responding to a question about public prayers at sporting events, she replied: "I think it's appropriate. In a group, one has a right to be silent. . . . You're not forcing anyone, those who want to can abstain . . . (What about non-Christians, such as Hindus or Buddhists? Might they not feel excluded?) [long pause] If the prayer is silent, it's OK. I have no problem with open prayer, but perhaps it's better for others to keep silent."

Respondents would often endorse what they thought were consensual government accommodations to religion but would alter their opinions when counterarguments were raised. In several instances (such as the conversation quoted above), respondents had some difficulty imagining that holiday displays would be controversial but were quick to adapt to additional information raising the issue of religious establishment.

Of course, some of these respondents may have been simply avoiding controversy by altering their verbal responses while still maintaining their positions. Yet this pattern of support for accommodation of practices when they were thought to be consensual, and opposition of accommodation that might be a source of conflict, seemed to be part of a deeper position that religion is a source of moral strength for a community when all agree but that religious conflicts are especially intense and should be avoided.

It is not surprising that many of those who supported accommodation on concrete issues changed their minds when alerted to the possibility of religious conflict. John Zaller (1992) and many others have noted that citizens generally respond to survey questions based on whatever considerations are readily accessible, but when they are primed to focus on other aspects of an issue, they frequently give a different response. Most of our survey respondents did not first consider the rights or sensibilities of religious minorities, or the possibility of religious conflict, because they most often interact with others who share their religious faith.

Essentially, our qualitative data revealed that most respondents favored government accommodation of religion in certain concrete issues because they regarded such policies as the expression of consensual beliefs. When confronted with the possibility of serious religious diversity, as the possible reaction of a member of a religion outside the Judeo-Christian tradition,[2] some changed their minds. This, of course, is quite consistent with the arguments made in chapter 1. Religious accommodation is most likely to seem attractive when religion is regarded as a source of social cohesion and consensus. Separationism is more easily endorsed when the potential for religious conflict is raised. The patterns of consistency and change in the focus-group data suggest that exposure to serious religious diversity is not part of the social experience of many Americans.[3]

It should be noted that some evangelicals we spoke with used a combination of free-exercise and communitarian rationales to justify their positions on some establishment questions such as school prayer, but their vision of community norms were generally limited to those of their own (largely evangelical) community. For example, one older evangelical man initially supported prayer in public schools, noting that the prayer need not be denominational but fit with the dominant religious group of the community. He was somewhat uncomfortable when confronted with the possibility of majority Catholic communities but stuck to his abstract position. But when the possibility of majority Buddhist school districts was raised, he took a different position: "Christian children should not be forced to hear prayers to a false god. Should Buddhist children be forced to hear prayers to the Christian

God? It wouldn't do them any harm . . . but I guess if they object, they could be excused from the room."

A third rationale that could lead respondents to favor separation in the abstract but accommodation on concrete issues would be more nuanced than our survey questions can determine. The Supreme Court has ruled that cities may display a nativity scene or a menorah so long as these religious symbols are part of a larger, secular display—including, for example, Santa Claus, a Christmas tree, and other nonreligious artifacts of the holiday season. Thus, at least some respondents may support separationist sentiments in the abstract, and like the Court majority they may also believe that these principles do not rule out all public displays of religious symbols if presented in the proper context.

So we cannot say from these data alone that most respondents to this survey exhibited inconsistent responses to the abstract and concrete items. Yet the fact that almost half of all respondents in the Williamsburg Charter data who supported separationist positions on both abstract questions supported the accommodationist position on *all* of the concrete questions suggests that at least some of those who supported no help to religion and a high wall of separation between church and state did not interpret these phrases in the manner in which they are commonly used in elite discourse.

Thus, there are two possibilities in resolving the discrepancy between abstract support for church–state separation and concrete support for accommodation. It is possible that respondents have nonattitudes in the church–state area and that these inconsistent responses merely reflect random responses. Alternatively, it may be that the public is responding in a meaningful way, either to the free-exercise element of some issues or to a presumed consensual element to religious observance or by displaying nuanced positions to complex issues.

Although we cannot test these alternative explanations directly, there are two indirect ways to sort between them. If the public is responding randomly to these items, then there should be no meaningful pattern to its responses to the concrete issues and, at best, a weak relationship between responses to the abstract and concrete questions. Moreover, the elites in the Williamsburg data should show a higher level of consistency. A meaningful set of attitudes, then, should exhibit an intelligible *structure*. It is to the existence or nonexistence of such structures that we now direct our attention.

The Structuring of Church–State Attitudes

Research on public opinion has generally shown that the public is not especially consistent in its opinions. Philip Converse (1964) established this lack of horizontal constraint (i.e., connections between opinions at the same level of generality) in the mass public, and although a variety of later studies have offered revisionist interpretations, there is general consensus among political scientists and sociologists that individual attitudes are not highly correlated in the mass public (Erikson, Luttbeg, and Tedin 1991).

Yet later research has also shown evidence of a surprising level of vertical constraint (i.e., connections between abstract principles and concrete issue positions) among the mass public (Conover and Feldman 1984; Hurwitz and Peffley 1987). For example, in the foreign-policy domain, Hurwitz and Peffley reported that "core values . . . are important determinants of individuals' preferences across a wide range of specific policies" (1987, 1113–14).

Vertical constraint arises from connections between abstract values and orientations and concrete-issue positions. For a few citizens, this constraint arises from a conscious attempt to apply their abstract values to political issues. Yet most citizens with constrained belief systems have not reasoned through the logic of the connection for themselves. Instead, political and social elites create packages of positions and communicate them to their followers. Various political and social groups endorse packages of issues that may or may not have logical links between abstract and concrete elements. Members of these groups learn to support the issue package of their group through socialization.

Discussions of the sophistication and constraint of the American public generally resemble arguments about the amount of Starbucks coffee in a mug. For some, it is interesting just how much coffee actually is in the mug while for others it is striking just how much of the mug is empty. Most empirical investigations of the structuring of public opinion find that the public does appear to distinguish between different types of issues, but many Americans hold packages of opinions that political scientists find to be inconsistent.

If the public is responding randomly to questions of religious separation, then we would expect very low correlations among responses to these items. To determine the level of horizontal and vertical constraint, we calculated gamma correlations between the items measuring abstract establishment orientations and concrete applications and among the various concrete questions. The results suggest that there is appreciable horizontal structuring to public sentiments on establishment questions.

In both surveys, the correlations are high for most questions. Only the question on Buddhist chaplains did not fit with the other concrete applications in the Williamsburg Charter data, doubtlessly because of religious particularism among Christians.[4] Although many Christians see Judaism as a cognate religious tradition (and Jews as the chosen people of their God), Buddhism is probably perceived as part of a larger set of "other" religious traditions.

For respondents to the Williamsburg Charter survey, the average gamma correlation between the various concrete establishment questions (excluding funding for Buddhist chaplains) listed in Table 4.1 was a substantial .48. The average correlation between the concrete applications and the abstract items was substantially lower—.31 for all concrete items with the high-wall question, and .28 for all concrete items and the question on government help for religion. A similar pattern was evident in the Washington area study. With five possible responses to each question instead of only two, we would expect the gamma correlations to be somewhat lower. The average correlation among concrete applications was .32. Once again the correlations were lower between responses to the abstract questions and concrete issue positions—.18 for the high-wall question, .20 for the help religion item, and .28 for government protection of the Judeo-Christian heritage. The latter abstract item was especially highly associated with attitudes on teaching of creationism and Judeo-Christian values in schools and on a moment of silence. Thus, respondents in both surveys were more likely to perceive a connection between different concrete applications of issues related to religious establishment than they were to make a connection between a particular application and an abstract principle.

What do these correlations mean in terms of concrete responses? Although 60 percent of respondents in the Williamsburg Charter survey who took both separationist abstract positions favored prayer in Congress, 83 percent of those who took accommodationist positions on both abstract items supported this public display of Christianity. Similarly, although 68 percent of separationists favored a moment of silence in public schools, 90 percent of accommodationists took that position. On some consensual issues such as funding for Christian chaplains and public displays of the nativity, the differences were smaller although the direction of the relationship was consistent.

These data suggest that the public does perceive a certain structure to the various concrete items and relates that structure to abstract principles of church–state separation. To determine the substantive nature of this structure, we used LISREL and factor analysis to identify the major dimensions of public attitudes on religious separation. We used LISREL with the data from the Williamsburg survey because for two pairs of items—the crèche and menorah and funding for Christian and Buddhist chaplains—the measurement error was correlated.[5]

With LISREL, it was possible to test various theories of how the public structures its attitudes. The statistical technique produced measures of how well a given theory fit the data. A variety of models were tested with the Williamsburg data, but two were of special interest. First, it is possible that the public sees all of these concrete issues as part of a single, underlying dimension of religious establishment. This single-dimensional model was an adequate fit to the data, suggesting that at some level the public does perceive the connections among various items.

Yet a better model posited three separate dimensions to establishment issues. The first dealt with public displays of Judeo-Christian religious symbols—public prayers and Christmas/Hanukkah displays. A second dimension dealt with those items that explicitly involve the use of public funds—funds for military chaplains and religious schools and tax breaks for church property.[6] A final set of issues involved public schools in religious socialization—a moment of silence, required teaching of Judeo-Christian values, and teaching of creationism. One item showed a strong association with two different dimensions: The public viewed allowing students to use school property after hours for religious groups to involve both financial and socialization issues.[7]

Because the Washington area survey used items with five categories instead of the dichotomies of the Williamsburg Charter survey, we have used factor analysis to determine the underlying structure to public responses. An exploratory factor analysis identified the same three basic factors as from the Williamsburg data: public displays of Judeo-Christian faith such as prayers at high-school football games and displays of the crèche and menorah; the use of public funds to support Christian and Buddhist chaplains; and issues relating to public schools, including a mandate to teach Judeo-Christian values, a moment of silence, the use of school rooms for meetings, and the teaching of creationism. Once again, the question on allowing student religious groups to meet on public school property also loaded on the public-funds factor.

Taken together, these analyses suggest that the public does not respond to questions on the religious separation and establishment at random but, rather, displays an interpretable cognitive structuring of these questions. Two different statistical techniques applied to two different datasets with different sets of questions and different question formats produced a similar structure, suggesting strongly that we have uncovered some basic dimensions of public sentiments. If public opinion on these issues is meaningful, then we should also find that attitudes are systematically related to the factors that we would expect to predict them—especially education and religion.

Sources of Public Attitudes on
Concrete Establishment Issues

We have constructed scales from the items that measured similar dimensions in each study.[8] These scales make it possible to examine social-group differences in attitudes in a more parsimonious fashion because there are thirteen separate items in Table 4.1. Each scale was constructed as the mean of the various concrete items, with higher scores representing greater support for separation between church and state. The scales measure public support for separationist positions in the areas of public religious displays, public funding of religious activity, and religion in public schools.

In chapter 3, we found that a number of demographic factors predicted abstract establishment sentiments, including education, income, age, sex, region, and race. We also reported that ideology, partisanship, denominational affiliation, religious doctrine, salience, and practice all influenced these abstract orientations. We now seek to determine how these factors influence concrete attitudes.

We have estimated separate OLS regression equations for each establishment scale in both the Williamsburg and Washington, D.C., data. The results for the Williamsburg Charter survey are presented in Table 4.3, the results for the Washington area survey in Table 4.4. The results are generally consistent in these two tables although there are some subtle differences.

Table 4.3

**The Sources of Support for Church–State Separation,
Williamsburg Charter Survey**

	Public Displays	Public Funds	Public Schools
Education	.04**	−.01	.05**
Income	.00	−.00	.00
Age	−.00*	.00**	−.00
Sex	−.01	.04*	−.00
Black	.03	−.01	−.00
Hispanic	.03	.02	−.06
Southern Resident	.03	.01	−.02
Ideology	−.04**	.00	−.02*
Partisanship	−.02*	−.01	−.03**
Evangelical Denomination	.01	−.01	−.01
Catholic	.02	−.06**	.04*
Jew	.30**	.00	.09*
No Religious Affiliation	.10**	−.02	.00
Evangelical Doctrine	−.04*	−.03*	−.06**
Religious Salience	−.10**	−.05*	−.09**
Frequency of Attendance	−.01	−.03*	−.01
Intercept	2.05**	1.94**	2.10**
N	1319	1327	1328
R²	.22	.10	.17

Note: Entries are unstandardized regression coefficients.
* $p < .05$; ** $p < .01$.

In both tables, those with higher levels of education were generally less supportive of religious accommodation although there were exceptions. In the Washington area survey, better-educated respondents were especially more likely to support funding for Buddhist chaplains but were also slightly more likely to support funding for military chaplains in general. In the Williamsburg Charter data, better-educated respondents were more likely than others to support public funding of private religious schools, and this reversed relationship canceled out some of the effects of education on the other items of the scale.

Precisely why better-educated citizens were somewhat more sup-

Table 4.4

**The Sources of Support for Church–State Separation,
Washington Area Survey**

	Public Displays	Public Funds	Public Schools
Education	.04*	−.11*	.17**
Age	.00	−.00	.00
Sex	.11	.25**	.03
Black	−.10	.50**	−.20*
Hispanic	−.07	−.04	−.13
Ideology	−.02	−.14*	−.17**
Partisanship	−.11**	−.03	−.08**
Evangelical Denomination	.02	−.12	−.02
Catholic	−.09	−.03	−.03
Jew	.13	−.03	.00
No Religious Affiliation	.19	−.04	.19
Liberal Christian Identity	−.19*	−.04	−.00
Fundamentalist Identity	.03	.13	−.13
Evangelical Identity	−.39*	.08	−.25**
Pentecostal Identity	−.02	−.01	−.16
Evangelical Doctrine	−.19	.30	−.35**
Spirit-filled Experience	−.27*	.03	−.40**
Attendance	−.20**	.10**	−.16**
Intercept	2.02**	2.14**	2.09**
N	335	326	326
Adjusted R^2	.23	.11	.16

Note: Entries are unstandardized regression coefficients.
*$p < .05$; **$p < .01$.

portive of public funding of religious schools is unclear. It may be that education ameliorates some of the anti-Catholic prejudice that may fuel some responses to the question. A number of less-educated evangelicals favored religious accommodation on every issue except spending on religious schools, and these respondents were the most likely to think that Catholics have too much influence on society. However, controls for anti-Catholicism did not eliminate this relationship entirely.

It is also possible that better-educated respondents respect the educational standards of Catholic schools and recognize their importance in providing quality education to some inner-city children. It may also be that graduates of Catholic schools are more likely to obtain a college degree and to retain a loyalty to their parochial education. Finally, better-educated citizens are more likely to send their children to private schools and therefore to support funding for such schools, regardless of their religious connections.

Other demographic factors showed a less consistent pattern. Age showed a weak but significant relationship in the Williamsburg data, with older citizens more supportive of public displays of Judeo-Christian religion but less supportive of using public funds on religious organizations or activities. This latter effect was primarily evident in lessened support among younger Americans for funding for military chaplains. Although our data did not provide a clear explanation for these phenomena, they did show that men who were of military age during World War II were the most supportive of funding for chaplains and young women were the least supportive. It may be that those who live through the horrors of combat may be more supportive of using public funds to pay for chaplains, regardless of their own religious views.

Blacks in the Washington area survey were significantly more likely to oppose the use of public funds to pay for military chaplains, and the difference was especially great for Buddhist chaplains.[9] They were also significantly more likely to favor a prominent role for Judeo-Christian teachings in the public schools. African-American leaders in Washington, D.C., pushed hard in 1994 for a ballot referendum for school prayer although ultimately their petition drive fell short of the required number of signatures.

Although blacks in the Williamsburg and Washington, D.C., surveys were not distinctive in their scores on the scales we used to measure support for public displays of Judeo-Christian symbols, in this instance the scales disguise some interesting variation. Blacks were significantly *less* likely than whites to favor displays of the menorah and significantly *more* likely to favor displays of the crèche. Blacks may especially oppose displays of the menorah because it is not a Christian symbol (much as they especially oppose public funding of Buddhist chaplains), but it is also likely that at least part of this result is because of anti-Semitism among some (though certainly not all) African Americans. In data from the 1988 American National Election

Study, blacks rated Jews significantly less favorably than non-Jewish whites, even after holding constant region, educational levels, religious doctrine, and religiosity. We will return to this theme in the next chapter.

Political variables also predict attitudes toward religious establishment. Conservatives and Republicans were more likely in both surveys to support establishment positions. This finding suggests that the mass public does respond to elite-level discourse on these issues. Since theologically conservative Christians have been most active in the Republican Party and have fought for conservative positions on a variety of lifestyle or "family" issues, it is not surprising that members of the mass public reflect these patterns.

Although demographic and political factors influence attitudes on establishment, religious factors provide the best explanation. Indeed, when we reestimated the equations in Table 4.3 with only the religious measures as explanatory variables, the goodness of fit was only slightly reduced. In other words, religious variables alone provide almost as good a predication of attitudes on church–state issues as the entire set of variables in Table 4.3.

In the Williamsburg Charter data, Catholics were distinctive in their support for public funds of religious institutions and practices and in their lower levels of support for Judeo-Christian values in public classrooms. Not surprisingly, Catholic support for public funding of religious institutions was most striking in support for religious schools. Catholics may be less supportive of mandated teaching of Judeo-Christian values in schools because they fear that in many regions of the country, an evangelical or fundamentalist religious orthodoxy would dominate classroom presentations. And Catholics were less supportive of teaching creationism because the Catholic church does not endorse a literal interpretation of the Genesis creation story.

Jews were distinctively less supportive of public displays of Judeo-Christian symbols, including the menorah, and more likely to oppose teaching creationism and Judeo-Christian values in public schools. Those with no religious affiliations were more likely to oppose public displays of religious symbols. Those who held evangelical doctrinal views were more likely to favor religious accommodation, as were those for whom religion is highly salient in their lives.

In the Washington area survey, the smaller sample meant that many substantial relationships were not statistically significant. As in the Williamsburg Charter data, Jews and those with no religious affiliation were more likely to oppose public displays of religious symbols, but here the relationships did not achieve the conventional standards of statistical significance. Those who identified as evangelicals were more likely to support public displays of religion and Judeo-Christian education in schools, and somewhat surprisingly those who identified as liberal Christians were also more likely to favor public displays of Judeo-Christian imagery. Further analysis revealed that these self-identified liberal Christians were almost exclusively African Americans, who may have been voicing their political leanings in their religious identification.[10]

Evangelical doctrine is associated with support for Judeo-Christian religion in public classrooms, and those with a pentecostal experience were significantly more supportive of accommodationist positions on public displays of religion and on religion in public schools. This latter relationship was especially strong among blacks. Other research (Wilcox 1992) has shown that African-American pentecostal and charismatic Christians in Washington are distinctively conservative on a number of issues, including abortion. Self-identified fundamentalists were not distinctive on any of the scales, but they were distinctive on two items that go into the scales: They were especially opposed to displays of the menorah and for funding of Buddhist chaplains. Finally, those who attend church regularly were more supportive of accommodation on all three scales.

Taken together, these data suggest that attitudes on concrete issues of religious establishment are primarily determined by religious factors and to a lesser extent by education. Highly religious evangelical and pentecostal Christians are the most supportive of accommodation while Jews and highly-educated, secular citizens are the least supportive. Catholics are somewhat wary of some aspects of accommodation but are especially supportive of funding for parochial schools.

Although scales are the easiest way to examine group differences in attitudes, they can occasionally conceal interesting patterns. Although we have discussed above some of the group differences on items that constitute each scale, it is useful to examine those differences directly. Table 4.5 shows the responses of members of the main religious traditions to each concrete issue. The general patterns fit those from the regression analyses, but there are some interesting patterns in this table. Note, for example, that there were no real differences among the members of the three main Christian traditions on many of the ques-

Table 4.5

Religious Sources of Concrete Establishment Opinions
(percentage of each group taking separationist position)

	Mainline Protestant	Evangelical Protestant	Catholic	Jew	No Preference
Prayer in Congress	20	15	35	73	57
Prayer in High School Sports	28	19	40	73	41
Manger Scene on City Land	12	11	12	61	25
Jewish Candles on City Land	14	13	14	57	27
Military Chaplains	5	6	7	7	14
Buddhist Chaplains	22	39	17	5	13
Government Funds for Religious Schools	69	51	43	65	63
Tax Church Property	53	50	52	56	69
School Rooms for Religious Meetings	27	25	24	40	29
Moment of Silence in Schools	18	13	19	43	40
Government Requires Teaching of Judeo-Christian Values	62	51	69	76	78
Teaching Evolution Only	12	5	12	40	23
Teaching Evolution and Creationism	78	73	83	56	75

tions—on whether cities can display nativity scenes or menorahs, on allowing student religious groups to hold meetings on school property, on tax breaks for churches, on the funding of Christian military chaplains.

Catholics were much less likely than Protestants to favor public prayers, however. Presumably this is true in part because they fear that these will be Protestant prayers (see especially Wills 1990). Yet Catholics did not object to a moment of silence in the classroom; indeed, even the small number of Jewish respondents were generally in favor of this form of silent prayer that can vary according to the religious traditions of the student although Jews were far less likely to support this than were Christians. Thus religious minorities were at least somewhat supportive of general religious accommodation but not of public displays of Protestant Christianity.

Catholics were more likely than the other two Christian groups to support public funds for religious schools, and evangelical Protestants were more supportive than mainline Protestants. More Catholics send their children to religious schools than evangelicals, and there are more evangelical religious schools than those associated with mainline denominations. Yet evangelicals were evenly divided on support for religious schools, and support was lower among those denominations in which religious particularism seems most common (Wilcox 1992; Jelen 1991a, 1993a). Fundamentalist and pentecostal respondents, who were more likely to have negative evaluations of Catholics, were less likely than those who attend more moderate evangelical churches to support aid to religious schools, probably in part because they do not want tax dollars to go to Catholic schools. These doctrinally orthodox Protestants may oppose funding of religious schools for a second reason—because funding comes with strings, including requirements for curriculum and teacher training. Support for funding religious schools was also lower among older evangelicals, those who did not hold evangelical doctrinal beliefs, and those who believed Catholics have too much influence on society. Evangelicals were more likely than the other groups to favor requiring public schools to teach Judeo-Christian values and to support teaching of only creationism. Yet support was quite high among all respondents for teaching creationism *and* evolution.

Finally, it is interesting to note that American Jews were the least supportive of public displays of the menorah, but were the single most supportive of funding Buddhist chaplains. With so few Jews in the sample, these relationships must be interpreted cautiously. Yet we will see in chapter 5 that among a larger sample of Jewish rabbis support for displays of the menorah was generally low but support for funding Buddhist chaplains was high.

It seems likely that some Jews reject public displays of the menorah because they are seen as opening the door to more frequent displays of Christian symbols at Christmas. One Jewish student told one of us that when communities display the menorah, "they are doing this so they can be even more blatant in their displays of Christian symbols." In addition, public displays of the menorah are seen as distorting the Jewish faith. One Jewish woman noted that "Hanukkah is a relatively minor Jewish holiday, yet because it falls close to Christmas and involves some gift-giving, it has been elevated out of proportion. Displays of the menorah are done for Christians, so that they can think of themselves as fair and neutral, not for Jews." Finally, many Jews may object to displays of the menorah because such public symbols are almost always included in a larger *Christmas* display, including Christian and other holiday symbols.

Yet Jews are far less likely to oppose funding Buddhist chaplains, perhaps because they see a clear benefit in a totally "nonpreferentialist" policy in that area. Military chaplains are not public displays of religion but instead provide private religious counseling for military personnel. A nonpreferentialist policy would also allow continued funding of Jewish rabbis in the military service.

Elite Attitudes on Religious Separation

We have found that although there is a substantial disjuncture between public attitudes toward religious separation in the abstract and the concrete, the public does seem to hold coherent sets of issue positions. Moreover, these attitudes vary systematically across levels of education, among different partisan and ideological groups, and across various types and levels of religious involvement. We conclude from these results that the gap between abstract and concrete sentiments is not primarily due to the cognitive limitations of average citizens, who simply cannot understand the concrete applications of the principles they espouse.

Instead, we argue that many may respond to elements of free exercise that are imbedded in some of these issues and that many respondents do not see public displays of the Christian manger scene or public prayers at high-school graduation ceremonies as involving a separation of church and state. Elites play a major role in determining the meaning of terms such as "separation of church and state" and "establishment," and the public may be taking their cues from these elites. Herbert McClosky and John Zaller (1984) have argued that when American elites are in consensus, the public generally shares that consensus. When elites disagree, however, the public is more likely to exhibit inconsistent beliefs.

Perhaps the apparent confusion concerning the applications of the establishment clause simply reflects that political, religious, and economic leaders do not agree on the meaning of religious establishment. If, for example, one set of leaders regards nativity displays as unconstitutional "establishment" but another group regards such exhibitions as perfectly legitimate expressions of majority sentiments of a given community, the notion of a "correct" meaning of religious establishment may make little sense. Thus, it is important to examine the attitudes of the elite groups on church–state issues to determine if they are sending mixed signals or if perhaps they are more supportive of religious separation in the abstract than in the concrete.

The multivariate analysis suggests that, in general, individuals with less attachment to religion and with higher levels of education were generally more supportive of separation between church and state than other Americans. The various elites sampled by the Williamsburg Charter had high levels of education, and several elite groups were less involved in religious practice than the general public. It seems likely, therefore, that the secular elites will be more supportive of the separation of church and state than was the general public, both in the abstract and in the concrete.

We expect that religious elites will differ greatly in their positions on these issues. Catholic priests, Jewish rabbis, and mainline Protestant ministers may favor an abstract high wall of separation between church and state, but evangelical Protestant ministers are likely to voice support for protecting a Judeo-Christian heritage. For Catholic priests and Jewish rabbis, a high wall of separation may be seen as a mechanism for preventing the Protestant majority from establishing their religious traditions while mainline Protestants may favor separation because of their ideological positions. Catholic priests are also likely to want to help all religions and especially to favor aid to religious schools.

The data in Table 4.6 generally support these expectations. The four groups of secular elites took separationist positions on both abstract issues: approximately two-thirds of business leaders, media gatekeepers, and government officials favored a high wall and no aid for religion, as did fully 86 percent of academics. Among the religious elites, Jewish rabbis and mainline Protestant ministers also supported separation in the abstract, but evangelical Protestant ministers and especially Catholic priests favored religious accommodation. A majority of Catholic priests favored not only government aid to religion, but also support for protecting America's Judeo-Christian heritage, a finding in marked contrast to Catholic members of the general public.[11] Nearly half of the priests took accommodationist positions on both abstract issues.

Table 4.7 shows the positions of each elite group on concrete establishment issues. Although members of these elite groups were strongly

Table 4.6

Elite Positions on Abstract Establishment Issues
(percentage of each group taking each position)

	Academics	Business	Media	Government
General Orientations				
No Government Help for				
Religion	89	80	67	79
High Wall of Separation	95	81	86	83
Combined Positions				
No Help/High Wall	86	69	63	67
Help/High Wall	8	11	20	14
No Help/Protect	3	11	5	11
Help/Protect	3	10	12	7
	Ministers	Priests	Rabbis	
General Orientations				
No Government Help for				
Religion	68	40	81	
High Wall of Separation	57	40	88	
Combined Positions				
No Help/High Wall	49	25	77	
Help/High Wall	12	14	10	
No Help/Protect	18	15	5	
Help/Protect	22	47	8	
	Mainline Protestant Ministers	Evangelical Protestant Ministers		
General Orientations				
No Government Help for				
Religion	77	63		
High Wall of Separation	69	47		
Combined Positions				
No Help/High Wall	60	37		
Help/High Wall	10	14		
No Help/Protect	12	24		
Help/Protect	18	25		

supportive of separation in the abstract, there was strong support for accommodation on many concrete issues. Even among the four secular elite groups, where support for separation in the abstract was strongest, there was general support for some accommodation to religion in public life and even for public funding for religion. A majority of all four groups favored funding Christian and Buddhist chaplains, opposed tax-

Table 4.7

Elite Support for Separation on Concrete Issues
(percentage of each group taking each position)

	Academics	Business	Media	Government
Prayer in Congress	75	32	45	31
Prayer in High School Sports	86	52	73	58
Manger Scene on City Land	59	19	36	26
Jewish Candles on City Land	60	18	38	25
Military Chaplains	14	6	3	9
Buddhist Chaplains	22	20	14	16
Government Funds for Religious Schools	76	68	73	69
Tax Church Property	48	42	38	35
School Rooms for Religious Meetings	41	26	38	30
Moment of Silence in Schools	75	32	52	47
Government Requires Teaching of Judeo-Christian Values	91	74	85	87
Teaching Evolution Only	68	18	30	28
Teaching Evolution and Creationism	32	72	65	69

	Ministers	Priests	Rabbis	Control
Prayer in Congress	12	10	56	54
Prayer in High School Sports	25	34	84	60
Manger Scene on City Land	11	9	85	23
Jewish Candles on City Land	16	8	83	22
Military Chaplains	8	3	2	5
Buddhist Chaplains	35	6	6	16
Government Funds for Religious Schools	64	17	64	66
Tax Church Property	11	7	23	60
School Rooms for Religious Meetings	20	14	70	30
Moment of Silence in Schools	22	15	75	34
Government Requires Teaching of Judeo-Christian Values	52	43	74	83
Teaching Evolution Only	13	7	43	25
Teaching Evolution and Creationism	72	89	56	70

ing churches, and favored allowing student religious groups to use school rooms to meet.

Academics were the most likely to support separation of church and state on concrete issues. Very large majorities opposed public prayer in Congress and at high-school sporting events, and majorities opposed public displays of religious symbols as well. Academics opposed the use of government funds for religious schools, the requirement that schools teach Judeo-Christian values, and a required moment of prayer. College professors were the only elite group to oppose teaching creationism in schools. On only four items did a majority of academics take accommodationist positions: on funding military chaplains (both Christian and Buddhist), on taxing church property, and on allowing the use of school rooms for religious meetings. Each issue also can be conceived as involving the free exercise of religion.

The other three secular elite groups took fairly similar positions although the media gatekeepers were somewhat more supportive than business or government elites of separationist positions. Business, government, and media elites favored allowing official prayers in Congress but opposed them at high-school sporting events. They were strongly supportive of public displays of Christian and Jewish religious symbols, of funding military chaplains, and of teaching creationism in schools along with evolution. Business leaders were as supportive of teaching creationism (along with evolution) as were Protestant ministers, and the other elite groups were almost as supportive.

Such strong support for the teaching of creationism among secular elites is surprising. As noted above, the question is worded in such a way as to indicate that teaching both is somehow more fair, but elites should be less swayed by this type of question wording than the general public. It should be noted that the question did not indicate *in which classes* creationism and evolution would be taught, nor did it suggest that both theories be given equal weight or credibility. It may be that some of these elite respondents would favor teaching creationism in biology classes as an equally probable alternative to evolution, but it is more likely that these elites would favor teaching creationism only in other classes (such as literature or history) or perhaps discussing the creationist argument in biology classes while noting that biologists are virtually unanimous in their belief in some form of evolution.

It is instructive to compare the responses of these secular elites to a similar set of respondents from the mass sample. We identified a group of 269 respondents from this latter group who had college educations, did not hold evangelical religious doctrine, and were only moderately involved in religious activity. The business and governmental elite groups were not markedly more separationist than this group of similarly well-educated, secular citizens. This suggests that much of the difference in support for concrete accommodation between these elite groups and the mass sample is explained by their higher levels of education and their lower levels of religious involvement.

Jewish rabbis also generally took separationist positions, and on some issues they were even more supportive of separationism than academics. They opposed public prayers and religious displays, including the display of the menorah. Indeed, rabbis were the elite group that was *least* supportive of public displays of the menorah on city land. Rabbis opposed government funds for religious schools, a moment of silence in the classroom, the teaching of Judeo-Christian values in the schools, and allowing student religious groups to meet on school property. They were strongly supportive of funds for military chaplains, however, and opposed to taxing church property. Slightly over half favored teaching creationism along with evolution, but no rabbi favored teaching only creationism. This latter finding suggests that many rabbis regard "equal time" provisions as involving either the free exercise of religion or more general issues of academic freedom. They may regard "creationism plus evolution" as accommodating the desires of religiously conservative parents, and thereby enhancing their rights of free exercise, while allowing students to "make up their own minds" (Martin and Jelen 1989). Moreover, rabbis may also be reluctant to interfere with the autonomy of classroom teachers, some of whom may desire to teach creationism as an alternative to evolution.

A majority of ministers and priests took accommodationist positions on most issues. They strongly favored public prayer and displays of religious symbols, funding for military chaplains, allowing schoolrooms for religious groups, a moment of silence in schools, and the teaching of creationism along with evolution, but they opposed taxing church property. A narrow majority of priests also favored requiring the teaching of Judeo-Christian values in schools, and an overwhelming majority favored providing government funds for religious schools. A majority of Protestant ministers opposed both of these latter positions.

Table 4.8 shows the evangelical–mainline split among Protestant ministers. On every issue, mainline Protestant ministers were more

Table 4.8

Evangelical–Mainline Split among Protestant Ministers, Support for Separation on Specific Issues
(percentage of each group taking each position)

	Mainline	Evangelicals
Prayer in Congress	17	6
Prayer in High School Sports	42	11*
Manger Scene on City Land	17	6
Jewish Candles on City Land	19	14
Military Chaplains	12	4*
Buddhist Chaplains	40	33*
Government Funds for Religious Schools	68	62
Tax Church Property	12	12
School Rooms for Religious Meetings	23	20
Moment of Silence in Schools	35	12*
Government Requires Teaching of Judeo-Christian Values	56	47†
Teaching Evolution Only	26	0*
Teaching Evolution and Creationism	61	82*
N	42	49

†$p < .10$; *$p < .05$.

supportive of church–state separation than evangelical ministers although the differences were not always statistically significant. The evangelical–mainline divide was largest on whether public prayers should precede high-school sporting events, whether there should be public funding for military chaplains, and whether schools should require a moment of silence or teach evolution.

These data suggest that although elites support church–state separation in the abstract, on specific issues they are likely to take accommodationist positions. Indeed, the business and governmental elite groups are not significantly more supportive of separation on many concrete issues than the general public although they are far more supportive of separation in the abstract.

Table 4.9 shows support for separationist positions on concrete issues among elites who took separationist positions on both abstract questions. For comparison, the figures from the general public initially shown in Table 4.2 are presented as well. There is a very large litera-

Table 4.9

Support for Separation on Concrete Issues among Elites Who Favor No Help to Religion and a High Wall of Separation

	Academics	Business	Media	Government
Prayer in Congress	80	36	54	39
Prayer in High School Sports	91	61	81	69
Manger Scene on City Land	66	25	47	36
Jewish Candles on City Land	68	25	46	33
Military Chaplains	15	7	3	6
Buddhist Chaplains	21	19	17	13
Government Funds for Religious Schools	83	72	86	75
Tax Church Property	50	48	40	40
School Rooms for Religious Meetings	46	26	55	36
Moment of Silence in Schools	80	37	69	58
Government Requires Teaching of Judeo-Christian Values	92	76	90	96
Teaching Evolution Only	71	23	36	37

	Ministers	Priests	Rabbis	Public
Prayer in Congress	20	37	64	40
Prayer in High School Sports	42	61	92	49
Manger Scene on City Land	13	19	93	19
Jewish Candles on City Land	22	14	93	21
Military Chaplains	12	8	2	8
Buddhist Chaplains	33	8	8	16
Government Funds for Religious Schools	73	35	85	75
Tax Church Property	16	20	25	62
School Rooms for Religious Meetings	24	39	73	19
Moment of Silence in Schools	30	36	88	32
Government Requires Teaching of Judeo-Christian Values	72	62	83	78
Teaching Evolution Only	24	7	50	21

(continued)

ture that consistently reports that elites show higher levels of vertical and horizontal constraint than the general public. These results lead us to expect a stronger vertical link between abstract establishment position on attitudes on concrete applications. What is striking in the data in Table 4.9, however, is that the elite groups did not exhibit a mark-

Table 4.9 *(continued)*

	Mainline Protestant Ministers	Evangelical Protestant Ministers
Prayer in Congress	30	5
Prayer in High School Sports	59	17
Manger Scene on City Land	17	6
Jewish Candles on City Land	21	22
Military Chaplains	17	5
Buddhist Chaplains	27	42
Government Funds for Religious Schools	76	69
Tax Church Property	13	21
School Rooms for Religious Meetings	21	28
Moment of Silence in Schools	44	6
Government Requires Teaching of Judeo-Christian Values	73	71
Teaching Evolution Only	41	0

edly higher level of apparent consistency between their abstract and concrete positions than the general public.

Academics and rabbis who supported separation on both abstract positions generally supported separation on concrete issues although both groups favored funding for military chaplains. Academics favored allowing student religious groups to meet in public school rooms (an issue that also involves free exercise of religion), and rabbis opposed taxing church property. On all other issues, these two sets of elites supported separation.

Yet a majority of business and government and even media elites who favored church–state separation in the abstract supported nativity scenes and menorahs on city lands, opposed taxing church property, and supported the teaching of creationism in public schools. Business and government elites favored allowing religious groups to meet on school property and Congress to start its sessions with a prayer. Business leaders also favored a moment of silence in schools.

Among religious elites, Protestant ministers and Catholic priests who endorsed separation in the abstract were even more likely to support religious accommodation on many concrete issues. Among ministers, the evangelical–mainline split was again evident. The data in this table might be compared with those in Table 4.7, which included *all*

Protestant ministers, not merely those who endorsed separation in the abstract. What is interesting in this comparison is that among those who endorsed separation, evangelical ministers were far more likely than mainline ministers to oppose funding Buddhist but not Christian chaplains and also to draw a distinction between nativity scenes and menorahs on city land. It is among those who voiced support for separation in the abstract that the particularism of evangelicals was most evident.

This high level of support for concrete accommodationist positions among elites who favored a high wall of separation and no aid to religion in the abstract is somewhat surprising. It provides strong evidence that the disjuncture between abstract and concrete positions in the general public is not due to their inability to reason from abstract to concrete.

Of course, it is possible that these results show that elites also sometimes display nonattitudes. Some of these individuals may have given little thought to these issues in the past and therefore may not have considered the connections between their abstract and concrete positions. Yet we suspect that these data show a more substantive pattern. Once again, some elites may see these issues as involving free exercise or believe that church–state separation applies only on conflictual issues. Others may be voicing their support for constitutional guarantees in the abstract yet see nuanced arguments for some of the concrete accommodationist positions. A moment of silence in which each individual may or may not pray to her god(s), as she chooses, is clearly not establishing a particular religion and if properly framed may not even establish religion over irreligion.

For all of these reasons, it is probably inappropriate to classify those elites who indicated support for a high wall of separation and support for some public role for religion as inconsistent. Rather, it is useful to note that among several elite groups, as among the general public, there exists a sizable number of citizens who support both separation of church and state in the abstract and at least a limited public role for religion in American society.

Elite Attitudes: Multivariate Analysis

It is possible that some of the differences among elite groups in support for free exercise or accommodation found in Tables 4.6 and 4.7

Table 4.10

Sources of Elite Support for Church–State Separation

	Public Displays	Public Funds	Public Schools
Media	.08*	.03	.01
Academics	.21**	.04	.11**
Business Leaders	.03	.05*	−.04
Evangelical Ministers	.02	.04	−.11*
Mainline Ministers	.07	.02	−.04
Priests	−.07	−.16**	−.22**
Rabbis	.47**	.11**	.11**
Sex	−.02	.09	−.02
Age	−.00	.00	.00
Region	.00	.01	−.00
Ideology	−.08**	−.02	−.06**
Partisanship	−.05**	−.03*	−.07**
Attendance	−.09**	−.05**	−.06**
Evangelical Doctrine	−.08**	−.03*	−.06**
Intercept	0.92**	1.03**	1.20**
N of Cases	779	783	782
R^2	.40	.21	.35

Notes: Entries are unstandardized regression coefficients. Elite groups are compared in this equation to government officials.
*$p < .05$; **$p < .01$.

may be due to differences in religious doctrine, religiosity, ideology, partisanship, gender, or age. In order to sort out the sources of elite attitudes on church–state separation, we estimated three OLS equations, using as dependent variables scales measuring attitudes toward public displays of religious symbols, public funds for religious institutions and practice, and religion in public schools. The results are shown in Table 4.10. We included dummy variables to identify members of various elite groups, with the excluded category government officials.[12]

There are some consistent differences among the elite groups. The media and academics were more supportive of church–state separation than government officials although the differences were not statistically significant for the use of public funds. It should be remembered that the Williamsburg survey was conducted in 1987 and that many government officials in this period would have been Reagan appointees. Business leaders were significantly less likely to favor the use of public funds to support religious practice or institutions.

Jewish rabbis were consistently more supportive of church–state separation, especially on public displays of Judeo-Christian symbols. Priests were consistently more supportive of accommodation, and this difference was especially pronounced on the use of public funds (primarily for religious schools) and on religious education. Mainline ministers were not significantly different from government officials on any scale while evangelical ministers were significantly more favorable toward religion in the classroom. The lack of distinctiveness of mainline and evangelical ministers may seem surprising, given the bivariate differences in Table 4.7. In this table, we control for church attendance and evangelical doctrine. In essence, we are then comparing evangelical ministers with evangelical government officials who attend church regularly. In this comparison, the ministers are unique only in their support for religion in the classroom. It is evangelicalism per se, rather than the status of an evangelical minister, that increases support for accommodation.

Ideology and partisanship were significantly related to all three scales, with Republicans and conservatives more likely to support church–state accommodation. Similarly, attendance and evangelical doctrine were significantly related to all three sets of attitudes, with evangelicals and those who attend regularly less supportive of separation of church and state.

Elite differences persist even after controls for religiosity, religious doctrine, ideology, partisanship, and demographic variables. Media and academic elites and Jewish rabbis were all consistently more supportive of church–state separation while Catholic priests were less supportive, even when we held constant differences in religious involvement and other factors.

Conclusions

Depending on one's level of optimism or pessimism about the quality of political thinking in the mass public, the results presented in this chapter suggest that the coffee mug is either half empty or half full.

The relationships between abstract attitudes toward religious establish-ment and concrete applications of these positions are of at least moder-ate magnitude and in the expected direction. The public does respond to these issues with apparently meaningful attitude structures although mass attitudes on concrete applications of religious accommodation are more differentiated than one might expect.

Conversely, many people are "abstract separationists" but "concrete accommodationists." That is, many are generally considerably more accommodationist at the applied level. This result may suggest that there is a lack of vertical constraint on the part of many members of the mass public. This pattern is also evident among elites. Although we expected to find that elites would show higher levels of apparent con-sistency between their abstract and concrete positions, in fact most elite groups shared with the mass public strong support for separation in the abstract and accommodation in the concrete. If mass publics take their cues from elites, then these results from the elite survey make the apparent inconsistency much less surprising.

There are several possible explanations for the apparent disjuncture between abstract and concrete cognitions. It may be that much of the rhetoric of church–state separationism is primarily symbolic. In chap-ter 1, we noted that separationists tend to view religion as a source of societal division and conflict. Separationists tend to use the rhetorical strategy of the "slippery slope," which suggests that once a relatively innocuous exception to the doctrine of church–state separation is per-mitted, the door is open for more offensive, egregious abuses by reli-gious majorities. For example, Levy (1986) uses the examples of blatant anti-Semitism and public Protestant prayers to illustrate the risks of religious accommodation.

However, members of a mass sample may focus on the particular concrete activity being depicted and may not perceive a risk of the erosion of the more general principle. As long as the particular activity in question does not seem to threaten conflict, many members of the mass public may approve, without concerning themselves with the risk of future abuses by religiously motivated groups. Indeed, our focus-group data make it clear that many respondents are unaware of the extent of religious diversity in the United States. Several respondents changed their accommodationist answers in a more consistent, separationist direction when confronted with the possibility that government accommodation of Christianity might be offensive to adherents of "authentic" but exotic religious traditions.

It is also possible that the effects of separationist attitudes at the abstract level may be overridden by attitudes about the free exercise of religion. That is, American citizens may believe that the principle of free exercise of religion, rather than religious establishment, is involved in the concrete activities depicted in this chapter. Again, our focus-group data suggest that the initial reaction of several respondents to issues of religious "establishment" is the concept of free exercise. Because we, as U.S. citizens, are entitled to "freedom of religion," why can government (an instrument of the popular will) not be used to advance religious values? To the extent that members of the mass public have not worked out the precise relationship between the establishment and free-exercise clauses, they resemble the U.S. Supreme Court.

Thus, the data presented in this chapter suggest that the mass public in fact has meaningful attitudes on issues involving questions of religious establishment. Substantively, these attitudes (at both the mass and elite levels) appear nuanced and varied. Attitudes about concrete applications are organized around the *type* of religious observance under consideration. The survey data suggest that it matters to the mass public precisely what sort of public activity is being contemplated. Is such activity costly (as is the case of issues involving taxation) or compulsory (an issue most likely to be salient in public schools)? Moreover, our focus-group data suggest that members of the mass public can be made aware of the possibility of religious conflict (and strongly desire to avoid it) but do not regard the mere *possibility* of religious disagreement as a sufficient reason to suppress the consensus of a particular community. The qualitative responses suggest that public accommodations to religion must offend real people (as opposed to violating an abstract principle) before such displays should be abandoned. Because few Americans are actively hostile to religious displays, and may have little direct experience with people from outside the cultural mainstream, the "harms" inflicted by the public accommodation of widely held religious values may seem largely hypothetical.

Our results also suggest that several values (including religiosity, church–state separation, religious free exercise, democracy, and civility) intersect when issues of religious accommodation are raised. Because most Americans probably desire all of these values, the precise policy preferences expressed may depend on the context in which the issue is posed. Both mass and elite samples seem to believe that multiple values are at stake with respect to questions of religious establishment and that no one value consistently overrides the others.

Notes

1. We also conducted question-ordering experiments using surveys in large introductory political-science courses at Georgetown and found approximately a 10 percent difference in support for funding Buddhist chaplains between instruments where the item appeared immediately after the question on Christian chaplains and one in which it appeared much earlier. The dropoff was smaller for displays of the menorah—approximately 5 percent.

2. The qualitative data revealed that such consideration was only granted to religions that might be regarded as part of a foreign heritage. Members of unorthodox "cults" or atheists were not generally deemed worthy of such protection.

3. It may be noteworthy that all of the above conversations took place in the Midwest, not in the Washington area.

4. Religious "particularism" refers to a belief in the exclusive authenticity of one's own religious tradition. For an analysis of this concept, see Glock and Stark 1966.

5. Because all of the items are dichotomous and several are quite skewed, weighted least squares is the most appropriate algorithm, using polychloric/polyserial correlations. The analysis in this chapter posited that the two pairs of items discussed above had correlated measurement error. Other correlated error was posited for contiguous items, items with identical wording, and items with similar reflection.

6. Of course, taxpayer funds are frequently involved in displays of the crèche or menorah. Yet these outlays are often small, and the question wording focused on the use of public land, not money.

7. It is interesting that the public sees this activity as involving public funds but does not appear to see the costs of using city land to display nativity scenes and the menorah. Possibly a few respondents see such Yuletide displays as good for business and therefore not involving a net loss of revenue because the government collects taxes on sales. Many probably do not consider the costs of maintaining these displays, of lighting them at night, and in some cases of purchasing and storing them. Of course, in *Allegheny County v. ACLU,* the crèche was owned by and put up by a private religious group, which paid for all costs of the display.

8. The public display scale exhibited a reliability (alpha) of .70 for the mass Williamsburg sample, .84 for the elite sample. For the funding scale, the alphas were somewhat lower: .32 for the mass, .40 for the elite. The scale dealing with religious accommodation with respect to school socialization had a mass alpha of .51, and an elite alpha of .66. For the Washington area survey, the alphas were .69 for the public display scale, .66 for the funding scale, and .65 for the school scale.

9. The fact that women and blacks were less supportive of funding for military chaplains may reflect their greater reluctance to support military funding more generally.

10. In other words, these liberal Democrats may say they are liberal Christians although they take doctrinally orthodox positions because the word liberal connotes politics to them.

11. It should be remembered that in southern Europe, the Catholic church has embraced an official endorsement by the state.

12. Government officials were the median group on the three scales. All coefficients are therefore interpreted as whether the elite group in question were more or less supportive of separation of church and state than government officials.

5

Attitudes toward
the Free Exercise
of Religion

In this chapter, we turn our attention from attitudes that appear to involve questions of religious establishment to those pertaining to the free exercise of religion. It seems reasonable to expect that attitudes toward religious free exercise will appear less consistent and sophisticated than those associated with the question of religious establishment. As we argued in chapter 1, the establishment clause has been the main axis of contention between separationists and accommodationists in legal discourse. Specifically, the main difference between the two opposing legal perspectives has been a dispute concerning the scope of the establishment clause. To the extent that mass opinion reflects public political controversy, this political clarity appears to have resulted in the simple, easily interpretable patterns reported in chapter 4.

We will see below that the concept of religious free exercise is a powerful symbol for many Americans, but the applications of the free exercise principle are seldom clear or free from extraneous considerations. As some of the focus-group material in the preceding chapter revealed, issues of religious free exercise are often intertwined with questions of religious establishment. In many concrete cases, the question of which religion clause is operative is precisely at issue. Are courts that deny purely religious holiday displays preventing unlawful religious establishment, or are they interfering with the free-exercise rights of the community? Do prohibitions on organized prayer in school constitute "coercion" of religious minorities and therefore constitute establishment, or are students being arbitrarily denied their right to pray, as those who favor school prayer would argue?

Further, applications of the free-exercise clause are confusing even when no establishment issue is involved. As noted in chapter 1, the meaning of the free-exercise clause is disputed even among legal accommodationists. A "libertarian" position on issues of free exercise would suggest that whatever limits are placed on religiously motivated behavior government cannot distinguish between creeds based on either their popularity or their content. Taoists, Buddhists, and perhaps even Satanists would be entitled to the same prerogatives and protections as Catholics, Methodists, or Baptists. By contrast, those who have a "communitarian" understanding of the free-exercise clause might argue that the clause has a purpose and that that purpose is to promote social cohesion and public morality. To that extent, it might well be argued that promoting religious freedom for groups that lie outside the cultural or religious mainstream might undermine the purpose of the free-exercise clause and render this portion of the First Amendment self-defeating.

The distinction between these understandings of the free-exercise clause become important because the issue of religious liberty is often posed in the context of protecting the religious prerogatives of unconventional sects or "cults." When courts or legislatures confront issues of religious free exercise directly, they often must determine whether Native Americans may use hallucinogenic drugs in religious ceremonies, whether oddly dressed and potentially disruptive Hare Krishnas may solicit money in public places, or whether Santerians may sacrifice animals to their gods. The rights of Roman Catholics to take communion, or of Baptists to conduct Bible study on Wednesday evenings, are simply not disputed in American politics.

A related set of issues regard the role of religious leaders in the political process. Although the Supreme Court overturned the few remaining state laws banning clergy from holding public office in 1978, the American public remains quite skeptical of political roles for religious leaders. When religious elites endorse candidates, mobilize their constituents, or run for office, are they simply exercising their rights as citizens, or are they bringing improper religious influence to bear on the "secular" realm of politics (see especially Greenawalt 1988)? Do the activities of such diverse people as Daniel and Phillip Berrigan, Jesse Jackson, Jerry Falwell, and Pat Robertson violate church–state separation?

Thus, questions of religious free exercise are rarely posed cleanly or directly in American politics. While most Americans clearly value the right to exercise one's religion freely in the abstract, publicly visible applications of the free-exercise clause are likely to be contaminated by questions of other legal rights, the identity of unpopular groups seeking religious freedom, or both. Our expectation, then, is that religious variables will not be nearly as helpful in explaining attitudes toward the free exercise of religion as they were in accounting for attitudes about religious establishment. We might well expect serious disagreement among people who themselves are quite religious or religiously orthodox about the nature of the right to exercise one's religion freely.

Abstract and Concrete Support
for Religious Free Exercise

The Williamsburg Charter survey contained no abstract free-exercise questions, but we did include two items in the Washington, D.C., survey. We first asked respondents whether "people have the right to practice their religion as they see fit, even if their practices seem strange to most Americans" and whether "it is important for people to obey the law, even if it means limiting their religious freedom." There was near unanimous support for an abstract right to practice even strange religion: 96 percent of the Washington area sample expressed agreement.[1] Only a minority of respondents favored civil disobedience for religious groups, however: 21 percent disagreed that citizens should obey a law that limited their religious freedom.

The overwhelming support for free expression of religion in the abstract suggests that many Americans view this as one of the most fundamental rights. That few would endorse civil disobedience is also not surprising, considering the range of possible conduct that could fall into that category.

In Table 5.1, we show the percentage of Washington area residents who supported free exercise on these abstract items and on several concrete applications. Although the public strongly favored support for free exercise for even strange religions in the abstract, the concrete application of these principles was considerably more limited. Although fully 96 percent said they supported freedom of religious exercise for even a strange religion, only 82 percent would allow students to wear

Table 5.1

Support for Religious Free Exercise, Washington Area Survey

	Percentage Supporting Free Exercise
Abstract	
Practice religion, even if it seems strange	96
Obey law, even if it limits religious freedom	21
Concrete	
Immigrants should convert	89
Allow religious headgear	82
Jews off on High Holidays	81
FBI (not) infiltrate Muslim groups	81
Allow religious leaders to picket porno shops	65
Conscientious objector status should be granted	55
Fundamentalists should preach on campuses	59
Native Americans should use peyote	58
Not require pledge of allegiance	44
Restrict Hare Krishnas in airports	40
Satan worship	35
Illegal cults convert teens	31
Allow animal sacrifice	28
Christian Scientist parents withhold medical treatment from their children	15

religious headgear to schools,[2] and only 28 percent would allow animal sacrifice, despite the detailed description of such practices in the Old Testament.

Yet overall, the data in Table 5.1 show a public that is generally accepting of religious practices that might seem to them to be unusual. Large majorities did not believe that immigrants should convert to Christianity, favored allowing children to wear religious headgear to schools, supported allowing Jews to take off from work on High Holidays, and opposed the FBI infiltrating all Muslim groups in the United States. Majorities also favored allowing religious leaders to picket stores where "pornography" is sold, allowing those whose religious views prohibit killing to claim a conscientious objector status to avoid military service, allowing fundamentalist preachers to speak on college campuses, and allowing Native Americans to use peyote in their religious services. In this latter point the public was more supportive of free exercise than the U.S. Supreme Court.

Washington area residents were almost evenly divided on whether

Table 5.2

Support for Religious Free Exercise, Williamsburg Survey, General Public

	Percentage Supporting Free Exercise
Stop Hare Krishnas from soliciting at airports	34
Ban Satan worship	35
Stop the Reverend Moon from publishing newspaper	56
Prohibit cults from recruiting teens	24
No place in United States for Muslims	71
FBI infiltrate cults	33
Religious groups should stay out of politics	32
Religious groups have legal right to be in politics	68
Moral Majority should stay out of politics	34
Churches should be denied tax exemptions if they prevent women from being priests/ministers	67
Television fundraising by religious leaders should be illegal	55
Jewish leaders fund pro-Israel groups	61
Religion is OK in right-to-life movement	56
OK if religious leaders support candidates	64
Religious leaders influence South Africa policy is OK	44
Religious leaders hiding illegal immigrants is OK	38
Religious leaders trying to close "pornographic" bookshops is OK	66

to require the pledge of allegiance of schoolchildren even if it violates their religious beliefs, and a small plurality favored banning Hare Krishnas from soliciting at airports. Washington area residents were generally opposed to religious free exercise that might harm humans or other members of the animal kingdom: Majorities opposed allowing Satan worship, allowing "cults" to convert teenagers, allowing animal sacrifice, and allowing Christian Scientist parents to withhold medical treatment from their children.

The Williamsburg surveys contained no general questions about religious free exercise but did pose a number of concrete applications involving religious liberty. The precise question wordings are contained in the appendix. As Table 5.2 shows, substantial majorities favored some applications of the free-exercise principle, but in no case did support for religious liberty approach unanimity.

We have divided the table into two sets of questions, the first pertaining to the free exercise of religious practice, the second about the role of religious groups and leaders in politics. The general public favored a role for Muslims in America and allowing the publication of a newspaper by the Reverend Moon (the *Washington Times,* not identified in the question). A majority favored banning Hare Krishna solicitations at airports, however, and large majorities favored banning Satan worship, allowing the FBI to infiltrate cults, and laws banning cults converting teenagers. The general public in the Williamsburg charter surveys appeared somewhat less supportive of free exercise than the Washington area residents, perhaps because of the higher levels of education of Washington residents and their greater exposure to religious diversity although differences in question format make such inferences tentative.

Majorities favored allowing religious groups to participate in politics, religious leaders to support candidates, Jewish leaders to fund pro-Israel groups, and religious elites to participate in the right-to-life movement. The public was more divided on allowing religious leaders to try to change policy toward South Africa,[3] suggesting that many Americans favor allowing religious leaders to endorse only those causes they personally support. For example, although black evangelical Protestants supported *both* an active role for clergy in picketing pornographic bookstores and in opposing apartheid, white evangelicals strongly favored the former but opposed the latter.

Finally, on two general questions that asked whether the respondent approves of religious groups in politics, large majorities wanted religious groups, particularly the now-defunct Moral Majority, to stay out of politics although majorities acknowledged the right of religious groups to be active. These latter figures suggest that many respondents were able to make a clear distinction between the legal rights of religious groups and their own personal preferences.

The Structuring of Attitudes on Free Exercise

In chapter 4, we found that the public organized its attitudes toward religious establishment in a comprehensible manner, differentiating between issues that involved public education, the use of tax dollars, and public displays of religious symbols. To determine the structuring of free-exercise positions, we performed confirmatory factor analysis using LISREL with the Williamsburg Charter data, and exploratory factor analysis of free-exercise items with the Washington area data. The concrete free-exercise questions included in these two surveys differed, so we did not expect to find an exact match in the structuring of attitudes. The Washington area survey had a wider variety of questions about freedom of religious practice while the Williamsburg Charter survey contained a large number of questions about the role of religious groups and leaders in politics.

Once again, we began by estimating a single-factor model in LISREL with the Williamsburg data to determine if the public perceived that all of these issues at one level involved an abstract freedom of religious practice. The fit was barely adequate, and a three-factor model fit the data far better. Exploratory factor analysis of the Washington area data also produced a three-factor solution.

In both surveys, one dimension tapped attitudes toward religious groups that might be considered dangerous or harmful. In the Williamsburg data, the questions constituting this dimension asked whether there should be laws prohibiting airport solicitations by Hare Krishnas, whether Satan worship should be illegal, whether the Reverend Moon should be stopped from publishing a newspaper, whether there should be laws prohibiting religious cults from recruiting teenagers, whether the respondent agreed that "there is no place for the Muslim religion in the United States," and whether the FBI should watch religious cults. In the Washington area survey, the items that loaded on this factor asked whether the FBI should infiltrate Muslim groups, whether there should be laws restricting the recruitment of teenagers to religious cults, whether Satan worship should be illegal, whether fundamentalist preachers should be allowed to convert young people on college campuses, and whether it should be illegal for Hare Krishnas to solicit money at the airport.

The common theme in these items was that the group in question might be considered in some manner dangerous. This was confirmed by many of the focus-group respondents. The following comments are illustrative. When asked whether laws should exist against Satan worship, An Episcopalian woman replied: "Yes, we should definitely prohibit Satan worship. I try to be fair. . . . But at some point, we've just got to say that some things are evil, and we don't have to put up with them."

An African-American pentecostal respondent elaborated on this theme: "Yes [should prohibit]. That's my religious perspective. I know that religious freedom is upheld by the Constitution, but that stops when my acts infringe on other people. (For example?) Well, I understand that Satanists practice human sacrifice and animal torture. [shudders] (Suppose they didn't do that?) Well, I'm not sure they'd be Satanists then."

The notion that some religious groups are actually harmful to their members was a common one among focus-group respondents. Asked whether there should be laws prohibiting cults from recruiting teenagers, the same pentecostal woman replied: "Teenagers aren't adults. . . . There's lots of influences out there that I'd want to protect my children from. (Like what?) Well, brainwashing, for instance. (What's the difference between brainwashing and persuasion?) I don't understand the question. (Suppose one of your children invited one of his friends to church?) [with increasing irritation] Are you saying my church is a cult! (I'm asking you what you think the difference is.) Well, I guess a cult demands total allegiance. . . . You forsake family, friends. . . . It's a total religion. My religion doesn't do that."

A Catholic woman who worked in medical research had a similar reaction to cults: "I'm interested in the methodology. Giving someone a pamphlet falls under free expression, throwing someone into a car is something else. . . . (Where would you draw the line?) Cults should follow the same regulations that the FDA requires for human subjects. (What are those?) Informed consent, no deception, description of all the risks, like that."

A Unitarian woman added the following: "It depends on how. Abduction or brainwashing should be illegal, but giving someone a booklet is OK. (How would you distinguish brainwashing from persuasion?) That's a hard question. [pauses] I guess I wouldn't let them do anything without the parents' consent. (Would you impose the same restriction on other churches?) No, [pauses] this makes me uncomfortable, I can't really say what the difference [between cults and churches] is, but it exists."

These comments illustrate rather graphically the tactics associated with religious cults in the minds of some members of the mass public. Terms such as "cult" or "Satanist" connote such practices as torture, human sacrifice, "brainwashing," and kidnapping. Although several respondents had difficulty distinguishing "brainwashing" from more mundane "persuasion," none had any doubt that the distinction could be made rather easily.

The "dangerous" theme did not seem to fit well with the question on Hare Krishna solicitations in airports although many respondents may have perceived that the group was likely to at least inconvenience citizens. As an older Catholic man told us: "Yes [airport solicitation should be illegal]. (Why?) Because those people are a pain in the ass."

An evangelical woman was less graphic, but no less clear in her condemnation of the practice: "We have the right not to be assailed. This is just the same as panhandling. (Don't Hare Krishnas have a right to express religion? Probably they think they're doing you a favor.) Other people, like salespeople, vendors, . . . need licenses, don't they? (Isn't religion different than selling brushes?) Well, people like that are trying to sell something, aren't they?"

Thus, there are a variety of religious groups regarded as harmful or dangerous by many people. Even the relatively innocuous experience of being solicited at the airport by a member of an exotic religious sect is characterized as "being assailed." Almost uniformly, focus-group respondents were unreceptive to the suggestion that the activities of these groups were in some sense protected by virtue of their religious character.

In the Washington area survey, a second dimension identified attitudes toward religious practices that might be considered unconventional but relatively harmless. These included allowing students to wear religious headgear "such as skullcaps and turbans" to public school, allowing Jews to stay home from work on the High Holidays, and allowing Native Americans to take the hallucinogenic drug peyote as part of their religious ceremonies.

Again, our focus group respondents indicated that these items were considered to be relatively innocuous religious practices. Several respondents had no problem with any of the activities in this list, but many had difficulty in conceiving these prerogatives as having an essentially religious nature. For example, one conservative Catholic male regarded the use of peyote as a privacy issue, without referring to the religious aspect of the controversy: "I'd make a kind of distinction between hurting yourself and hurting someone else. . . . As long as they're not hurting anyone . . . (How?) I'd be real nervous if they were driving [cars] while on the stuff. . . . You have the right to refuse government protection. . . . Actually, I think drugs should be legalized anyway."

A middle-aged evangelical woman was among several who saw the

peyote issue as one of tribal self-determination: "Is this on the reserva-
tion, or off? (Why would that matter?) Unless I heard wrong, I think
tribal law supersedes U.S. law."

A younger Catholic woman voiced similar sentiments: "Did the
practice come before the law, did it predate drug laws? (Why would
that matter?) I think if this were a historically established practice, that
would be an argument for protecting it. Some practices go back before
civilization."

Those who opposed the legal use of peyote had some difficulty with
a religious exemption from an otherwise valid law (the issue in *Smith*).
As a young Catholic male put it: "You have an obligation to obey the
laws of your country. . . . Your country gives you this religious freedom we've been talking about. . . . If we don't support the laws, there
won't be any freedom for anybody." (Suppose the Native Americans
regard their obligation to their god or gods as more important?) [im-
patiently] Look, the way it's supposed to be, at least in theory, we're
able to change the laws. . . . If these people don't like the drug laws,
for whatever reason, they should get off their . . . duffs and change
them."

Clearly, this respondent had some difficulty accepting the notion of
a permanent religious minority, powerless to affect national policy and
entitled to a special exemption from the law for religious reasons.

Focus-group respondents were generally supportive of the right of
schoolchildren to wear religious headgear to school. Even when the
issue of a dress code violation was raised,[4] respondents had some
difficulty taking the question seriously. An Episcopalian women argued: "(Should religious headgear be permitted?) [surprised] Sure,
why not? (Suppose the school wants to curb gang activity?) If that
headgear is part of who they are, what's the difference? I think this
would only be a problem for somebody hung up on separation."

An older Methodist woman voiced a similar sentiment: "They're not
hurting anybody. Children are the harshest critics, and if someone's
faith is strong enough to put up with the stuff that kids say to each
other, more power to them."

A final dimension of free-exercise attitudes in the Washington area
data included three items that seemed to tap what might be termed
religious xenophobia. Washington area residents were asked whether
people had the right to practice their religion "even if their practices
seem strange to most Americans," whether the FBI should infiltrate

Muslim groups, and whether immigrants should "be encouraged to convert to Christianity" because "America is a Christian nation."[5]

In the Williamsburg Charter data, the two final factors focused on the role of religious groups and leaders in politics. The second dimension, which we have termed religious groups, measured attitudes toward the propriety of political involvement by religious groups. The questions asked whether the respondent would prefer religious groups stay out of politics, whether such groups have a legal right to engage in political activity, and whether the Moral Majority, specifically, should stay out of politics. A third dimension tapped the extent to which religious leaders should engage in political activity at a more specific level. Respondents were asked whether it was appropriate for Jewish leaders to raise money for pro-Israel politicians, whether right-to-life activists should use religious arguments, whether it was appropriate for religious leaders to support political candidates, and whether it was appropriate for religious leaders to attempt to influence U.S. policy toward South Africa.

In the Williamsburg data, four items did not fit neatly into the three principal dimensions. Attitudes toward religious elites attempting to close "pornographic" bookshops or hiding illegal immigrants were not closely associated with other attitudes on activities by religious elites, presumably because the former elicits concern about the free expression of the book dealers and the latter involves breaking the law. In addition, attitudes toward tax exemptions for churches that deny women ordination and toward a possible ban on television fundraising by religious figures were also unrelated to other items. They are not included in the scales discussed below.

Thus, our initial analyses of both the Williamsburg and Washington area surveys suggests that public attitudes toward issues involving the free exercise of religion are varied and complex. As might be expected, people make distinctions based on the unfamiliarity of the group in question, the perceived threat posed by unconventional religious activity, and the specific activity in which religious actors are thought to be engaged.

The structuring of these attitudes seems quite sensible and suggests again that many members of the public hold real attitudes on these issues. The public structures its attitudes on free expression according to the nature of the group involved, supporting free exercise for those groups it does not consider dangerous and opposing free

Table 5.3

Free-Exercise Scales by Abstract Support for Religious Liberty, Washington Area Survey

	Dangerous Religion	Harmless Religion	Immigrant Religion
Obey Law	2.81	3.53	3.96
Neutral	2.98	3.59	4.14
Religious Liberty	3.19	3.96	4.08
Overall	2.90	2.38	4.00
N	533	531	533

Note: High scores indicate greater support for religious free exercise.

exercise for groups it considers possibly harmful. In both surveys we have constructed three scales from the various items that loaded on these factors.

Is there a relationship between attitudes toward abstract conceptions of religious free exercise and concrete applications of this principle? We can answer this question for the Washington area data, which included abstract and concrete free-exercise items. The data in Table 5.3 show the mean scores on the three free-exercise scales for those who believed that individuals should obey the law even if it meant limiting religious freedom, for those who took the opposite position, and for those who were neutral.[6]

Respondents who endorsed "obeying the law" at the expense of religious freedom were noticeably less supportive of the free-exercise rights of adherents of "dangerous" religions, as well as those of people who practice unconventional but "harmless" religions. The abstract free-exercise item was apparently unrelated to attitudes toward the religious liberty of immigrants.

These data show that public opinion on free exercise of religion is constrained both vertically and horizontally. Those citizens who think that religious freedom is so important to occasionally justify breaking the law are more likely to favor free exercise of dangerous and unusual religious groups, suggesting that abstract principles do constrain concrete positions. In addition, the public distinguishes among free-exercise issues based on the apparent danger of the groups and activities involved.

Table 5.4

Sources of Support for Abstract Religious Free Exercise, Washington Area Survey

Education	.03
Age	−.01
Sex	.12
Black	−.13
Hispanic	−.04
Ideology	−.11†
Partisanship	.04
Evangelical	−.16
Catholic	.00
Jew	.03
No Religion	.33†
Liberal Religious ID	−.03
Evangelical ID	.16
Fundamentalist ID	.57*
Pentecostal ID	−.12
Evangelical Doctrine	.09
Spiritual Experience	−.04
Church Attendance	−.02
Intercept	1.55
Adjusted R^2	.06
N	314

Note: Entries are unstandardized regression coefficients.
$†p < .10$; $*p < .05$

The Sources of Abstract and Concrete Positions

To determine the sources of abstract positions on religious free exercise, we have estimated logistic regression equations similar to those in chapter 3. Table 5.4 contains the results of a multivariate model, designed to explain responses to the second abstract free-exercise question, which raises the issue of possible conflict between obeying the law and practicing one's religion. The model accounts for only 5 percent of the variance, suggesting that other factors are needed for a complete explanation of these attitudes. One possible explanation for the limited explanatory value of these variables is that respondents may visualize different kinds of extra-legal activity when answering the question. Some liberal respondents may think of firebombing abortion clinics or even murdering abortion providers, or they may call to mind images of black clergy sitting at a segregated lunch counter. Those who visualized anti-abortion violence would be more likely to favor obeying the law than those who visualized civil-rights protests. Similarly, conservatives might think of Catholic priests pouring blood on draft records during the Vietnam war or of evangelical clergy picketing a pornographic movie theater. The disjuncture between support for a political role for clergy in picketing pornographic bookshops and in opposing apartheid suggests that citizens may accord protection for activities of which they approve, and deny that protection for similar activities that they oppose.

The model shows that women and respondents with no religious preference are slightly more likely to endorse "obeying the law" than are other respondents. The only religious variable that is significantly related to the abstract free-exercise item is fundamentalist self-identification. People who call themselves fundamentalists, regardless of denominational affiliation, are more likely to support religious liberty, even when it involves breaking the law. This finding, of course, supports previous research, which suggests that fundamentalists are most likely to hold attitudes of religious "separatism" and to make clear distinctions between the sacred and the secular realms (see Jelen 1987; and Smidt 1988). It is also of interest that education (typically the strongest predictor of attitudes toward issues involving civil liberties) is *not* significantly related to responses to this item.

In Tables 5.5 and 5.6, we show the sources of concrete attitudes on free expression. The data in Table 5.5 show that in the area surrounding the District of Columbia, religious variables are virtually irrelevant in accounting for attitudes toward the First-Amendment rights of "dangerous" religious groups. Older respondents and those with higher levels of education were more supportive of extending legal protection to dangerous religious groups while women, Hispanics, and self-identified conservatives were generally less supportive.

The failure of religious variables to explain variation in support for free exercise by "dangerous" religious groups suggests that many Americans do not see these questions as primarily religious issues but rather ones of community security. Many of our focus-group respon-

Table 5.5

Multivariate Analysis of Support for Free Exercise, Washington Area Survey

	Dangerous Religion	Harmless Religion	Immigrant Religion
Education	.10*	.11**	.21***
Age	−.01***	−.01***	−.00*
Sex	−.20***	.03	.05
Black	−.02	−.46***	−.11
Hispanic	−.40†	−.18	−.27
Ideology	−.08†	−.11*	−.15***
Partisanship	.01	.04	.04
Evangelical	−.18	−.03	−.31***
Catholic	−.00	−.13	−.03
Jew	.27	.49†	.24
No Religion	.22	−.04	.06
Liberal Religious ID	−.02	.03	.14*
Evangelical ID	−.00	−.12	.00
Pentecostal ID	−.13	.39***	.28*
Fundamentalist ID	.16	−.12	−.13
Evangelical Doctrine	−.09	−.12	−.09
Spiritual Experience	−.12	.10	.29**
Church Attendance	.01	.04	−.06*
Intercept	3.78	2.40	3.72
Adjusted R^2	.11	.19	.33
N	335	335	335

Note: Entries are unstandardized regression coefficients.
†$p < .10$; * $p < .05$; **$p < .01$; ***$p < .001$.

dents invoked the "harm principle" (Barry 1990): People should be free to engage in a wide range of behaviors as long as no harm to others is done. As noted above, several focus-group respondents believed that Satanists and cults in fact do harm their members. When pressed to distinguish between harmful behavior and mere adherence to a religious creed, most expressed skepticism that members of "cults" or "Satan worshippers" would ever refrain from harmful activity.

By contrast, religion is important in explaining attitudes toward the

Table 5.6

Multivariate Analysis of Support for Free Exercise, Williamsburg Survey, General Public

	Dangerous Religion	Religious Leaders	Religious Groups
Education	.10***	.07***	.01
Income	.03†	.02	.00
Age	−.00***	−.00***	−.00**
Sex	−.07***	.01	.00
Black	.06†	.09***	.13***
Hispanic	−.06	.06	.01
Region	−.02	−.00	−.03
Ideology	−.01	.00	.03†
Partisanship	−.01	−.01	.01
Evangelical	−.01	−.04	.03
Catholic	−.04*	−.03	.04
Jew	.05	−.04	.00
No Religion	.01	.00	.02
Church Attendance	−.00	−.01	−.01
Religious Salience	−.03*	.05**	.08***
Evangelical Doctrine	−.04**	.04***	.04*
Intercept	1.19	1.28	1.79
Adjusted R^2	.18	.08	.09
N	1326	1319	1317

Note: Entries are unstandardized regression coefficients.
†$p < .10$; *$p < .05$; **$p < .01$; ***$p < .001$.

free-exercise rights of adherents of "harmless" religions and of immigrants. Jews were more likely to support the free-exercise rights of these groups, and the relationship was not confined to the item that measured support for Jewish work exemptions on High Holidays. Self-identified charismatic and pentecostal Christians were significantly more supportive of free exercise for "harmless" groups while blacks were significantly less supportive.

Religious variables also influenced attitudes toward "immigrant" religious groups. Respondents who identified as "liberal Christians" were likely to support the free-exercise rights of immigrants, as were self-identified political liberals. Again, charismatic or pentecostal self-identification was strongly related to a willingness to tolerate the unconventional religious practices of immigrants; respondents who attended evangelical churches or who attended religious services frequently (regardless of denominational affiliation) were less supportive of such activity. Further, respondents who reported spiritual experiences, such as speaking in tongues, healing by faith, or "being slain in the Spirit," were also likely to support the First Amendment prerogatives of immigrants to the United States.

The distinctively lower levels of support for free exercise of "harmless" religious groups among African Americans was primarily due to the high levels of black disapproval of allowing Jews to miss work on High Holidays, a finding that echoes African-American opposition to displays of the menorah discussed in chapter 4. Blacks were not significantly less likely to favor allowing religious minorities to wear distinctive headgear to schools or to oppose the use of peyote by Native Americans.

The strong levels of support by self-identified charismatic and pentecostal Christians for free exercise by non-Christian groups is somewhat surprising. Elsewhere we have reported that those who attend pentecostal churches in the United States are the least tolerant of the rights of unpopular minorities of both the right and left to speak in communities, teach in colleges, or to write books that appear in public libraries (Wilcox and Jelen 1990). Why, then, in Washington, D.C., were self-identified charismatics and pentecostals *more* tolerant?

In Washington and its surrounding suburbs, pentecostal churches attract a somewhat different kind of adherent than is true nationwide. Especially in the Virginia and Maryland suburbs, growing pentecostal churches such as the Assemblies of God attract affluent, well-educated congregants. In addition, our measure asked respondents whether they consider themselves as pentecostals or charismatics, and charismatics who attend mainline Protestant or Catholic churches are also disproportionately well-educated and affluent. White respondents in the Washington area survey who identified as a pentecostal or charismatic were better educated than other whites.

Yet we control for education in this analysis, and pentecostals are more supportive of the religious rights of non-Christian groups regardless of their levels of education. One other characteristic of Washington area pentecostal churches may account for this result. Pentecostal churches in the white Washington, D.C., suburbs appeared to be more likely than other churches to rent their buildings to immigrant congregations. Thus, a pentecostal Christian may leave his Sunday service as members of a Korean or Hispanic congregation are arriving. It is possible that this exposure to immigrant groups who share a Christian faith may help mold more tolerant attitudes toward immigrants in general.

In contrast, pentecostal and charismatic churches in the African-American neighborhoods of Washington, D.C., seldom rent their buildings, and these predominantly black churches often preach the importance of black pride and of black identity. Black pentecostals were slightly less likely than other blacks to support the free-exercise rights of non-Christian groups. Thus, race interacts with religious identity and experience to shape attitudes toward free-speech rights of non-Christian groups.

Thus, the analyses of attitudes toward "harmless" and "immigrant" religious groups in Table 5.5 suggest that religious attributes play a complex role in shaping attitudes. Members of evangelical churches were especially supportive of limiting the religious freedom of immigrants while white pentecostals were especially likely to support religious liberty for all groups that they deemed as not dangerous.

The results for the Williamsburg Charter data in Table 5.6 show that religion has only a modest, but statistically significant effect on attitudes toward free exercise of "dangerous" groups. Catholics were somewhat more supportive of the free-exercise rights of "dangerous" religions while respondents who attached high importance to religion, as well as those who held evangelical beliefs, were somewhat less supportive. Catholics may have been more sympathetic to the claims of religious minorities because of their own history of minority status. Those with higher levels of education and income were more likely to support the free-exercise rights of these groups while women and blacks were not as likely to extend the protection of the First Amendment to such groups.

The second and third column in this table show the sources of support for political involvement by Judeo-Christian groups and leaders. Respondents for whom religion was highly salient, and doctrinal evangelicals as well, were generally supportive of the rights of religiously motivated people to engage in political activity. Evangelicals were especially supportive of political activity by the Moral Majority and of religious leaders picketing pornographic bookstores. Self-identified conservatives were slightly more supportive of political involvement by political groups, especially the Moral Majority.

Older respondents were more supportive of free-exercise rights on both the religious groups and religious leaders scale, as were African Americans. This latter finding is not surprising because black clergy and churches played a vital role in black politics during the civil rights movement and continue today to be important political institutions and leaders.[7]

Elite Perspectives on Religious Free Exercise

The general public responds to questions about the free-exercise rights of religious minorities by determining first its evaluation of the group itself. If the group appears to present a threat to humans or other animals, it is not supportive of protection of religious practices. If the group is considered harmless or involves immigrants, a majority favor freedom of religious practice, but attitudes vary in a complex way across religious groups.

This, of course, is not a new insight. It has been suggested that support for civil liberties is often organized around a group-specific heuristic (Sullivan, Pierson, and Marcus 1982). More generally, numerous studies have shown that group identifications and affect are very common means by which people organize political information (see Jelen 1993b; Conover 1984; Brady and Sniderman 1985; Sniderman and Tetlock 1986).

Why should this be so? Group attitudes provide a convenient way for ordinary people to classify and retain political information (Miller, et al. 1981; Tajfel 1970, 1981; Converse 1964). The political world is complex, and people are likely to devote most of their time and energy to nonpolitical pursuits, so some sort of cognitive "shorthand" is quite useful to citizens seeking to make sense of the discourse of public life.

It might seem as though this kind of reasoning is unsophisticated, representing the elevation of prejudice over principle. Yet some research has suggested that group-based heuristics require a moderate amount of political information and so are more often found among the best-informed members of the mass public (Sniderman, Brody, and Tetlock 1991). If this is true, then we may find the same group-based distinctions on free-exercise issues in the elite samples that exist in the general public.

It is also possible, however, that political elites will be somewhat less likely to apply different standards to religious groups based on their affective reaction to them. Elites may be more likely to apply abstract rules consistently than the general public. Indeed, many scholars have argued that elite attitudes are the strongest source of support for civil liberties in the United States. The general public may approve of stripping an unpopular minority of its rights, they argue, but elite consensus on the rules of the game and on individual rights prevents the mass public from acting on its prejudices. Several analysts (Schumpeter 1950; Lipset 1960; and Berelson, Lazarsfeld, and McPhee 1954) have argued that ordinary citizens are likely to exhibit authoritarian tendencies and to be ignorant of and therefore uncommitted to the norms of democratic procedure. Given this possibility, one can regard the lack of participation on the part of the masses as fortuitous (see Sullivan, Pierson, and Marcus 1982, 18; Berelson, Lazarsfeld, and McPhee 1954; Prothro and Grigg 1960) or support political arrangements that keep certain highly volatile issues off the public agenda (Dahl 1982; Lijphart 1975).

In order to distinguish between these possibilities, it is necessary to examine the Williamsburg elite survey. Table 5.7 shows support for each of the concrete applications of religious free exercise by elite group. The data contain few surprises but do not support the notion that there exists a consensus on religious free exercise at the elite level. In some instances—for example whether there is a place in the United States for Muslims—support for free exercise was virtually unanimous across elite groups. However, other issues were more controversial.

Academics, media elites, and rabbis were the most supportive of the free-exercise rights of unconventional religious groups, while business elites and Christian clergy were less supportive. Conversely, ministers and priests were most supportive of political involvement by religious groups with government elites the least supportive of such activity. Media elites were noticeably less supportive of the right of the Reverend Moon to publish a newspaper while Catholic priests were very suspicious of allowing religious leaders to support political candidates. A majority of rabbis and secular elites preferred that religious groups stay out of politics.

In order to gain a clearer sense of elite differences, we have combined the free-exercise responses for elites into the three scales described above for the Williamsburg survey of the general public. Our

Table 5.7

Elite Support for Religious Free Exercise, Williamsburg Survey, Elite Sample
(percentage taking free-exercise positions on each issue)

	Academic	Business	Government	Media
Stop Hare Krishnas	77	48	62	70
Ban Satan worship	89	69	75	82
Stop Moon newspaper	98	91	90	54
Prohibit cults from recruiting teens	83	59	66	66
No place for Muslims in United States	100	96	95	100
FBI infiltrate cults	93	73	77	85
Religious groups should stay out of politics	22	21	29	40
Religious groups have legal right to be in politics	81	68	69	74
Moral Majority should stay out of politics	69	63	73	66
No tax exemptions if sex discrimination	73	84	80	78
Ban television fundraising	91	82	88	87
Jewish leaders fund pro-Israel groups	93	86	89	90
Religion OK in right-to-life movement	87	81	79	71
Religious leaders support political candidates	89	76	75	72
Religious leaders influence South Africa policy	91	73	85	80
Hiding illegal immigrants is OK	53	25	34	36
Closing "pornographic" bookshops is OK	63	62	69	65

(continued)

examination of the structure of these responses suggests that elite organization of free-exercise attitudes is quite similar to that which characterized the mass public. A LISREL model suggests that the same three factors that characterized the mass data provide the best fit for elites as well, showing that elite attitudes are no more consistent or "constrained" than those of non-elite respondents. Moreover, the reliabilities for the elite scales that result from this factor analysis, while still robust, are slightly lower than those associated with the mass sample.[8]

Table 5.7 *(continued)*

	Ministers	Priests	Rabbis
Stop Hare Krishnas	54	51	65
Ban Satan worship	52	55	69
Stop Moon newspaper	79	84	87
Prohibit cults from recruiting teens	53	54	53
No place for Muslims in United States	87	97	96
FBI infiltrate cults	52	61	63
Religious groups should stay out of politics	64	62	40
Religious groups have legal right to be in politics	85	84	76
Moral Majority should stay out of politics	68	67	51
No tax exemptions if sex discrimination	86	95	94
Ban television fundraising	80	79	84
Jewish leaders fund pro-Israel groups	87	88	90
Religion OK in right-to-life movement	82	89	90
Religious leaders support political candidates	78	56	77
Religious leaders influence South Africa policy	74	85	90
Hiding illegal immigrants is OK	28	58	38
Closing "pornographic" bookshops is OK	83	93	66

Elites appear to conceive of free-exercise issues in a similar manner as the mass public.

How do elite groups differ in the content of their attitudes? Table 5.8 shows the position of each elite group on the three free-exercise scales. Academics and media elites were most supportive of the free-exercise rights of people whose religious beliefs and practices might be considered dangerous. All three groups of Christian clergy were the least supportive of religious freedom for such groups, with mainline ministers being somewhat less tolerant than either priests or evangelical ministers. Academics were the most tolerant of political activity on the part of religious leaders, followed closely by rabbis. Government and media elites were *slightly* more tolerant than Christian clergy, but the differences were quite minor.

Table 5.8

**Support for Religious Free Exercise by Occupation,
Williamsburg Elite Survey**

	Dangerous Religion*	Religious Leaders*	Religious Groups*
Academic	1.90	1.90	1.58
Business	1.72	1.78	1.51
Government	1.78	1.82	1.57
Media	1.83	1.82	1.59
Ministers	1.62	1.81	1.72
Evangelical	1.57	1.80	1.74
Mainline	1.67	1.80	1.71
Priests	1.67	1.79	1.69
Rabbis	1.72	1.86	1.55
Overall	1.76	1.82	1.59

*High scores indicate greater support for free exercise.

It is surprising that the largely secular academics were more supportive of political involvement by religious leaders than religious elites themselves. The differences were largest on support for a prophetic role for clergy on South Africa and for Jewish rabbis funding of pro-Israel politicians, but academics were also quite supportive of religion in the right-to-life movement and of religious leaders picketing pornographic bookshops.

It may be that academics were more likely than other elites to consider the abstract principles of these concrete applications rather than their emotional responses to the groups involved. There is some indirect evidence for this. Recall from chapter 4 that academics who held abstract separationist positions were far more likely than other elite groups to support separation on concrete issues. In addition, there is some evidence in these data that academics saw a single issue of free exercise. When we estimate the single-factor LISREL model for academics only, we get an acceptable fit, suggesting that many academics viewed freedom of religious exercise as a principle that transcended the nature of the religious groups involved.

The relative intolerance of Christian clergy for political activity on the part of religious leaders may have theological roots. Many clergy are reluctant to endorse political involvement on the part of religious leaders. Some ministers are fearful of negative reactions on the part of the laity to political activity (see especially Hadden 1969) while others regard politics as much less important than the task of promoting individual salvation (Jelen 1993a). Responding to a question about Pat Robertson, a Baptist minister told one of us, "I can't for the life of me understand why a man would give up the most exalted calling in the world—preaching the Gospel—just to try to achieve political office."

Finally, all three groups of Christian clergy were the *most* tolerant of political activity by religious groups. Although large majorities in each elite set believed that religious groups have a *right* to be involved in politics, many expressed a personal preference that they not exercise this right. Not surprisingly, evangelical clergy were the most supportive, followed by mainline clergy and then by priests. Rabbis and all three groups of secular elites were less supportive of religious-group involvement in public affairs than any group of Christian ministers. Business leaders and rabbis were the least tolerant on this scale, followed closely by government, media, and academic elites.

Overall, these data suggest that support for the free exercise of religion is contingent on the identity of the group seeking religious freedom for elites as well. Christian clergy were very unlikely to support such rights on the part of non-Christian, potentially dangerous religions but were more tolerant of political involvement by Judeo-Christian elites and groups. Conversely, academics and media elites preferred that conservative religious groups stay out of politics (though they acknowledged their right to involvement) but were the most supportive of all elite groups of the free-exercise rights of "dangerous" religions.[9]

It is also of some interest to compare the responses of mainline and evangelical Protestant ministers. Table 5.9 shows that mainline clergy were more supportive of the rights of Hare Krishnas to solicit in airports and were more likely to disagree that there is no place for Muslims in America. Mainline ministers were less likely to believe that the FBI should infiltrate religious cults and more likely to endorse Jewish support for pro-Israel groups and religious leaders seeking to influence U.S. policy toward South Africa. Similarly, mainline ministers were much more supportive of hiding illegal immigrants than were evangelicals. By contrast, evangelical ministers were more likely to support the right of the Reverend Moon to publish a newspaper (*The Washington Times* is a conservative paper) and to endorse political

Table 5.9

Ministerial Positions on Free-Exercise Issues by Evangelicalism, Williamsburg Elite Survey
(percentage of each group supporting a free-exercise position)

	Mainline	Evangelical
Stop Hare Krishnas	60	49
Ban Satan worship	53	51
Stop Moon newspaper	75	83
Prohibit Cults from recruiting teens	55	51
No place for Muslims in United States	98	76*
FBI infiltrate cults	62	41
Religious groups stay out of politics	60	67
Religious groups have legal right to participate in politics	85	84
Moral Majority stay out of politics	70	66
No tax exemptions if sex discrimination	84	88
Ban television fundraising	83	77
Hiding illegal immigrants is OK	40	15*
Closing "pornographic" bookshops is OK	84	81
Jewish leaders fund pro-Israel groups	91	83
Religion OK in right-to-life movement	80	83
Religious leaders support political candidates	75	81
Religious leaders influence South Africa policy	81	66

$*p < .05.$

involvement on the part of religious groups. On other free-exercise issues, mainline–evangelical differences were either small or nonexistent.

In chapter 4, we found that evangelical ministers were consistently more accommodationist on issues of religious establishment. On free-exercise issues, evangelical ministers were less supportive of the free-exercise rights of non-Christian groups. On many issues, however, there was no difference in the attitudes of evangelical and mainline clergy.

Thus, religious professionals are not consistently the most supportive of religious liberties. This is also evident when we hold constant other variables. In Table 5.10 we show the results of multiple regression analysis of the sources of elite opinion on free exercise. These data offer scant support for the hypothesis that religion or religiosity promotes general support for religious liberty. First, no religious vari-

Table 5.10

Multivariate Analysis of Support for Free Exercise, Williamsburg Elite Survey

	Dangerous Religion	Religious Leaders	Religious Groups
Region	−.06**	.01	.02
Age	−.01**	−.01**	−.01*
Sex	−.14***	−.07**	−.06†
Ideology	.06**	.05**	.02
Partisanship	−.01	.03	−.00
Church Attendance	.00	−.02*	−.04
Evangelical Doctrine	.00	−.02	−.02
Media	−.01	−.03	−.00
Academic	.03	.08*	.01
Business	−.09**	−.03	−.07†
Mainline Minister	−.12**	−.00	.02
Evangelical Minister	−.22***	−.06	.08
Priest	−.17**	−.08†	.07
Rabbi	−.16***	−.01	−.06
Intercept	1.93	1.02	1.82
Adjusted R^2	.17	.05	.06
N	783	782	782

Note: Entries are unstandardized regression coefficients.
†$p < .10$; *$p < .05$; **$p < .01$; ***$p < .001$.

able was significantly related to attitudes toward political involvement on the part of religious groups among the elite sample.

Religious variables did have some moderate effects on elite attitudes toward political involvement on the part of religious leaders. However, the effects of being a Catholic priest and of frequent church attendance were negative: Priests and frequent church attenders (regardless of occupation) were less likely to support the rights of religious leaders to engage in political activity.

Perhaps the most surprising result in Table 5.10 is contained in the equation explaining elite attitudes toward "dangerous" religions. *All* groups of clergy were much less supportive of religious liberty for unconventional religions than secular elites.[10] Although religious elites would seem to have a direct stake in the principle of religious liberty (indeed, perhaps a greater interest in such issues than other people), many of the religious members of the Williamsburg elite sample were quite willing to deny free-exercise rights to members of religions that lie outside the Judeo-Christian tradition. This finding characterizes the attitudes of rabbis and priests as well, despite the fact that such clergy represent denominations with a history of separation from the dominant Protestant culture. Although such elites were more tolerant of the free-exercise rights of adherents of "dangerous" religions than were members of the mass public, it seems clear that the effects of higher education and social status were offset to some extent by religious convictions. Religious elites presumably viewed these groups as likely to lead Christians and Jews astray from the true faith, and the danger posed by these groups outweighed their claim to free religious expression.[11]

Conclusions

Our analyses of attitudes concerning the free exercise of religion exhibit both similarities and differences with the account of attitudes toward religious establishment contained in chapter 4. In both cases, attitudes toward church–state issues were varied and complex at both the mass and elite levels. Support for free-exercise rights, as well as attitudes toward specific government acts in which issues of the establishment of religion might be raised, depended quite heavily on the circumstances under which these principles were presented to respondents. Again, the attitude structures of both establishment and free-exercise issues were quite similar for elite and mass samples.

In chapter 4, we showed that attitudes toward issues involving questions of religious establishment tended to be organized around *activities* in which government at various levels might be engaged. Respondents appeared to make distinctions between educational issues, issues involving government funding, and those questions affecting public displays of religious sentiment. By contrast, free-exercise attitudes tended to be loosely organized around the identities of *groups* seeking to make use of religious liberty. This group-based heuristic of free-exercise attitudes came through very clearly in the analyses of the Washington area survey and also seemed to underlie the structure of attitudes discerned in the Williamsburg data as well. While public attitudes on the establishment of religion appeared to be focused on *what* is being done by government in the religious sphere, free-exercise attitudes seemed to be based on *who* is engaged in religious activity.

Finally, there were important differences in the effects of religious variables on church–state attitudes as well. While chapter 4 revealed that most religious variables had the effect of increasing acceptance for "benevolent" government assistance to religion, the analyses in this chapter suggested that the effects of religion on free-exercise attitudes were both more limited and more complex. Religious variables were virtually irrelevant in accounting for variation between respondents on some of these attitudes. In other cases, religious observance or ortho-doxy appeared to be a source of theological particularism rather than of generalized support for free exercise.

These findings, in turn, suggest that many Americans hold "commu-nalist" values toward free exercise. That is, religious freedom may be regarded as an instrumental value, which might have the effect of increasing social cohesion and public morality. To the extent that the religious freedom of certain groups does not advance the achievement of such social goals, such liberty seems to be considered much less valuable.

Notes

1. As will be shown below, the use of the term "Americans" in this item appears to connote questions of immigration to some respondents. This item loads quite heavily on a factor relating to the free-exercise rights of immigrants.

2. That 14 percent of respondents would allow strange religious practice but deny the rights of schoolchildren to wear religious headgear may speak volumes to the limitations of the vision of some Americans.

3. The Williamsburg surveys were conducted in 1987 when the South-African policy of apartheid was still a prominent issue in international politics.

4. At the time of this writing, some school districts in the Chicago area had established dress codes in an effort to control street-gang activity.

5. Some of the focus group respondents were quite willing to make explicitly assimilationist arguments. For a sample of these sentiments, see chapter 3.

6. We chose this item because the other abstract item was essentially a constant.

7. It may seem surprising that blacks, who tend to be liberal Democrats, would favor the involvement of groups such as the Moral Majority in politics. Yet research has shown that many blacks are potential supporters of the Christian Right, and a few actually support Christian Right organizations (Wilcox 1991a). Allen Hertzke (1993) has shown that blacks were a potential constituency for Pat Robertson. Once again, blacks were slightly less likely to favor a political role for

Jewish leaders and surprisingly were not especially supportive of a role for clergy in criticizing U.S. policy toward South Africa.

8. The alpha coefficients for the elite scales were .65 for the dangerous religions scale (as opposed to .70 for the mass sample), .50 for the religious leaders scale (.55 for the mass public), and .58 for the religious group scale (.66 for the mass public).

9. Because the scales were computed using different numbers of items, we cannot compare across categories very easily. Thus, it is difficult to determine, for example, whether academics were more or less tolerant of the rights of religiously dangerous groups than of those of religious leaders. We can compare down the columns of Table 5.3 but not across the rows.

10. For the occupational dummy variables, government leaders constitute the comparison category.

11. It is also possible that some religious leaders have had experience with religious "cults," perhaps in counseling parents of young people who have joined these religious movements or in dealing with former cult members who have returned to the flock.

6

Conclusion

In this chapter, we explore some of the implications of our results for the practice of religious politics in the United States. Although few Americans have occasion to think seriously about church–state relations on a regular basis, we have shown that most of our respondents appear to have coherent, if somewhat nuanced, attitudes on such issues. While the structure of attitudes on the public face of religious expression does not come close to resembling a "proreligion/antireligion" dimension, there appear to exist underlying rationales for the distinctions drawn by the public. Moreover, our analyses of the elite samples of the Williamsburg studies suggest that the apparent complexity of mass attitudes on issues of church–state relations resembles (and may result from) correspondingly differentiated attitudes on the part of political, economic, educational, and religious elites.

In this concluding chapter, we return to the theoretical themes developed in chapter 1 and assess the empirical adequacy of the typology of church–state positions elaborated there. Do citizens take the sorts of positions defined by attitudes toward issues of religious establishment and free exercise? Do the positions on issues of church and state taken by mass publics correspond to the categories defined in chapter 1? What are the characteristics of people occupying each cell of the church–state typology?

Two Faces of Religious Accommodation

In chapter 1, we noted that there are two general rationales for an accommodationist understanding of the establishment clause. In one case, a reading of the First Amendment that allows for nonpreferential governmental assistance to religion is necessary if Americans are to be allowed the right of religious free-exercise. Government, by this understanding, is one means by which citizens can act on their religious beliefs. It is, from this free-exercise perspective, somewhat arbitrary to proscribe such policies as school prayer, holiday religious displays, and the like if those actions are favored by a majority of citizens who wish to practice their religion in these ways.

Many analysts of church–state relations have approached the question of religious accommodation from this free-exercise perspective. For example, in his recent book, *The Culture of Disbelief,* Stephen Carter argued for an expansive reading of the free-exercise clause, suggesting that "the religions, to be truly free, must be able to engage in practices the larger society condemns" (1993, 34). Carter included such practices as housing discrimination against unmarried couples, gender discrimination within religious denominations, and the withholding of medical treatment from children for religious reasons as being among those prerogatives that must be protected for the sake of religious autonomy. Moreover, Carter singled out the *Smith* decision for specific criticism, arguing that to allow otherwise legitimate acts of legislation to limit the religious prerogatives of believers is to undermine the basis of religious liberty and thus to violate the free-exercise clause.[1]

Carter went on to argue that such solicitous protection of religious free exercise is necessary precisely because religion has an important *political* role to play as social and political critic. An important public function of religion is to serve a "prophetic" purpose (Leege and Kellstedt 1993). As Carter asserted, "Democracy is best served when the religions are able to act as independent moral voices interposed between the citizen and the state, and . . . our tendency to try to wall religion out of public debate makes that role a harder one to play" (1993, 16). Carter cited the civil rights movement as an example of the positive role religion has to play in the public arena and suggested that democratic politics is deprived of an important moral voice (or voices) when religion is excluded from the making of public policies by an expansive reading of the establishment clause.

A related argument is that religious involvement in the public square is an essentially defensive reaction to government policies that make adherence to religious principles more difficult. Government (particularly the courts and other "unrepresentative" officials) is thought to enact policies that pose obstacles to the free exercise of religion. As Ralph Reed, head of the Christian Coalition, has put it, "[Religious political activism] is best understood as an essentially defensive struggle by people seeking to sustain their faith and their values. . . . They are far less interested in legislating against the sins of others, and far more interested in protecting their own right to practice their religion and raise their children in a manner consistent with their values" (1994, 18). Thus, it is often argued that practices such as teaching evolution or sex education in public schools work against parents seeking to raise children as orthodox Christians and therefore constitute a violation of religious liberty. Nor are such violations limited to the field of public education. Hubert Morken (1994) has argued that laws designed to protect homosexuals from employment or housing discrimination in fact violate the free-exercise clause by "coercing" economic interaction with people whose lifestyles may be considered sinful by doctrinally conservative religious people.

A second rationale for an accommodationist reading of the establishment clause is more communitarian in nature. Again, as noted in chapter 1, some modern analysts, such as Peter Berger and Richard Neuhaus, have followed Tocqueville in arguing that successful democratic politics requires a religious or moral basis. A general consensus on religious principles provides an ethical background within which democracy can operate. As Carter has put it, "Indeed, Tocqueville claimed, American was 'the place where the Christian religion has kept the greatest power over men's souls.' In Tocqueville's view, this meant that liberty was tempered by a *common morality*. . . . Translating Tocqueville's observations to the present day *(and removing his pro-Christian bias)*, one therefore sees two chief functions that religions can serve in a democracy. First, they can serve as the sources of moral understanding without which any majoritarian system can deteriorate into simple tyranny, and, second, they can mediate between citizen and the apparatus of government, providing an independent moral voice" (1993, 36; emphasis added). This passage is revealing because it suggests that it is possible for religion(s) to assert a "common morality" without restricting the range of permissible religious beliefs and practices. In Carter's opinion, a very expansive view of the free-exercise clause (including permitting practices that would otherwise be illegal) is compatible with a "priestly" public role for religion, in which religious belief provides the basis for a moral consensus.

Can Tocqueville's insight be retained while "removing his pro-Christian bias?" Such compatibility between religion's "prophetic" and "priestly" functions would seem to depend crucially on an empirical claim, namely, that there are no important doctrinal or moral differences between the various religions practiced in the United States. The accommodationist case assumes that religious belief is in fact a source of social cohesion and not a source of conflict. Such an assumption is, to say the least, controversial. Some recent research (Jelen 1991a; Wilcox 1992; Green 1993) has suggested that religious particularism (defined as negative affect toward people outside one's own denomination or religious tradition) has reduced the effectiveness of attempts to translate religious values into public policy. Indeed, the influence of the Christian Right figures such as Jerry Falwell and Pat Robertson in the 1980s was limited because both figures drew from relatively narrowly defined religious constituencies. The anti-Catholicism that has characterized much of the rhetoric of evangelical Protestantism, as well as public splits between fundamentalists and charismatics (see especially Wilcox 1992), has inhibited the formation of potentially formidable religious coalitions. The fact that both Christian Coalition leader Ralph Reed (1994) and James D. Hunter (1991) have devoted considerable effort to describing a "new ecumenism" suggests that people sympathetic to a strong public role for religion have perceived the fragmenting effects of religious particularism and are seeking to overcome this problem. If, in fact, people disagree seriously about such matters, agreement on the appropriate public expressions of religious values might be quite difficult and produce conflict and instability.

Reed's call for an ecumenical movement of Christian social conservatives appears to have borne some fruit. Mark Rozell and Clyde Wilcox (forthcoming 1996) have reported that among Virginia's Republican activists, the Christian Coalition is supported by fundamentalists, pentecostals, charismatics, many mainline Protestants, and a surprising number of Catholics. They cited one Catholic Christian Right activist in northern Virginia as noting that "we have formed relationships of mutual respect and even personal friendship which I suspect would have been unthinkable between Catholics and evangelicals twenty years ago." Yet there is evidence of lingering particularism in their data as well: Fundamentalists were noticeably cooler toward Catholics than were other Republican activists and somewhat cooler as well

toward Robertson, whose connections to the pentecostal wing of orthodox Christianity were especially evident in his home state of Virginia.

The ability of politically active leaders to form and maintain ecu-
menically diverse coalitions of "orthodox" (Hunter 1991) citizens will
be among the most fascinating questions of the next period in American political history. Whether people committed to traditional morality
from different religious traditions will be able to work together in
organizations such as the Christian Coalition is an empirical question
that will be answered when Minerva's owl flies at dusk. However,
there may be reasons to suggest that such ecumenical coalitions may
be inherently unstable. Roger Finke and Rodney Stark (1992) have
pointed to the utility of considering the competition between denominations for adherents in any larger understanding of religious activism.
That is, denominations in religiously diverse environments have incentives to attract and retain members quite aggressively. A corollary of
this economic model of religious "consumerism" is that it may be
rational for religious bodies to distinguish themselves from their com-
petitors to as great an extent as possible. In the long run, this sort of
theological "product differentiation" seems likely to increase religious
particularism, especially because churches compete for adherents
among loosely defined theological blocs. The hostility exhibited by
fundamentalist leaders in the early part of the twentieth century toward
pentecostals can be understood as part of a larger competition for the
same pool of potential recruits.

For example, if an American Baptist congregation needs to compete
for members, the pastor may have an incentive to explain to the laity
precisely how the American Baptist church differs from the Assembly
of God church a mile away or even from local congregations associated with the Southern Baptist Convention or the General Association
of Regular Baptist Churches. This might well require emphasizing
doctrinal differences that might seem quite minor to someone from
outside the tradition. Indeed, some recent research has suggested that
this sort of very precise doctrinal differentiation is quite common
among doctrinally conservative churches (see Jelen 1993a).

Thus, if religious services are, in some sense, the "site" of religious
socialization, religious learning that takes place in local congregations
might undermine the ecumenical tendencies of a group such as the
Christian Coalition. This is not to suggest that a religiously based
coalition of social conservatives is not possible but only that such a

grouping, like other interest groups and social movements in American politics, will have to deal with formidable centrifugal forces.

Even if the divisive effects of religious prejudice can be overcome, it is by no means clear that there exists even an *ethical* consensus among American Christians. At the elite level, there are clear differences between mainline and evangelical clergy. Many observers (Hadden 1969; Quinley 1974; Jelen 1993a) have shown that mainline clergy tend to be more interested in such "peace and justice" issues as homelessness, militarism, and racial discrimination than their evangelical counterparts. Moreover, the governing bodies of some mainline denominations have taken relatively liberal positions on issues of gender role differentiation and sexual morality (Ostling 1991). At the mass level, research has suggested that there exists substantial support for such "nonfamily" values as feminism and abortion rights among some devout, evangelical Christians (Wilcox 1989; Wilcox and Cook 1989; Cook, Jelen, and Wilcox 1992). And although conservative positions on issues of personal morality are associated with church attendance in virtually all Christian denominations, it has been suggested that few members of the laity hold anything approaching ideological "worldviews" on such matters (Jelen 1990). Even among committed, conservative Christians, there is a tendency to view such issues as abortion, homosexuality, creationism, and sex education on an ad hoc basis without apparent reference to a coherent underlying belief system. Thus, even shifting the focus of religious political activity from doctrine to morality may not be sufficient to hold together a coalition of diverse preferences.

Finally, it must be admitted that the nominal consensus on a Judeo-Christian heritage has been waning throughout the late twentieth century. Recent waves of immigration to the United States have included substantial numbers of people from Africa and (especially) Asia, and many of these immigrants are not Christians or Jews. Combined with the rise of "New Age" religions and a slow increase in the numbers of secular Americans, this trend suggests that the extent of religious diversity in the United States is increasing rapidly. Ecumenical coalitions of the religiously orthodox might well need to include Buddhists, Muslims, and Hindus (see Hunter 1994). Perhaps more important, protection of the free-exercise rights of such believers seems likely to undermine the priestly, consensual nature of American religion.

What all this suggests, of course, is that there may be an increasingly visible tension between the two rationales for the public accommodation of religious beliefs. To the extent that accommodationism is valued as an adjunct to the free exercise of religion, the range of religions entitled to public accommodation can be expected to increase. Conversely, religious accommodation as a means of providing a broad agreement on religious or moral principles within which democratic politics can be conducted may entail restricting the free-exercise rights of those whose religious values fall outside a presumed religious (or ethical) "consensus."

Patterns of Church–State Attitudes:
An Empirical Overview

To what extent can an empirical examination of public attitudes toward church–state relations illuminate the potential tension between the two bases for religious accommodationism? While our data do not permit us to settle all of the issues raised above, we can offer some preliminary analyses of public attitudes on such questions.

In chapters 3, 4, and 5, we have discussed separately public opinion on abstract and concrete issues of religious establishment and free exercise. This approach enabled us to look closely at the structuring and sources of opinions on issues relating to the two clauses of the First Amendment. Our separate analysis of these sets of issues makes political sense as well. Historically, elite debate has treated establishment and free exercise as separate sets of issues, with far more attention paid to the former than the latter. Moreover, we noted in the preface that most controversies surrounding accommodation versus separation deal with the dominant religious culture (Christian nativity scenes, Judeo-Christian prayers at high-school graduations) while many of the controversies surrounding free exercise center on the rights of religious minorities (Native Americans who wish to use peyote in religious rituals, immigrants who wish to sacrifice animals).

Yet it remains clear that many establishment issues have clear implications for free expression of religion. Moreover, conservative elites are increasingly phrasing their arguments in favor of accommodation in the language of free exercise. Issues such as voluntary school prayer are depicted by one side as involving an establishment of Christianity and by the other side as involving the freedom of schoolchildren to pray. Indeed, proponents of school prayer routinely emphasize its "voluntary" nature (Chapman 1991).

It is useful, therefore, to consider the intersection of these two sets of attitudes. In chapter 1, we proposed a four-fold typology of ideal positions on church–state issues, and we can use the data in this book to see if all four types of positions exist among the general public. In both the Williamsburg mass sample and the Washington, D.C., survey, the scales on free exercise are correlated with one another, and the scales on establishment are also correlated with one another. This suggests that the public sees the various issues of establishment as related and sees the various issues of free exercise as related.

The data also suggest that there is a weaker association between attitudes on establishment and free exercise. In the Washington, D.C., data, which have better measures of free-exercise opinion, those who were most supportive of religious accommodation for Christian groups were the *least* supportive of free-exercise rights of non-Christian religious minorities who were perceived as dangerous or involving immigrants. Similarly, in the Williamsburg survey of the general public, those who were most favorable toward public displays of Judeo-Christian symbols were also those most likely to favor restricting the free-exercise rights of "dangerous" religious groups. This relationship also held for each group in the Williamsburg elite survey and for every religious, educational, or demographic group we examined. Those who wanted public prayers at high-school sporting events were the most likely to want to stop Hare Krishnas from soliciting at airports. Those who opposed such prayers were the most likely to be tolerant of the Krishnas.

The correlations between our measures of various free-exercise and establishment issues are relatively robust and suggest that at least some of the political and academic debate on church–state issues has mischaracterized the nature of the dispute. These issues are frequently seen as pitting those who favor a public role for all religion versus those who do not—the "Godly" against the "Godless," the "orthodox" versus the "progressives," or in our typology the religious non-preferentialists against the seculars.

In chapter 1, we suggested that elite debate on both establishment and free-exercise issues can be organized into two camps for each First Amendment clause: accommodationists versus separationists for establishment issues, communitarians versus libertarians for free exercise. From these positions we created a four-fold typology of elite positions. Christian preferentialists favor public displays of religious symbols but oppose the free exercise of non-Christian religious minorities. Religious nonpreferentialists favor allowing religion a place in the public square and favor allowing all religious groups to participate. Religious free-marketeers wish the government to be neutral between religions and between religion and no religion. They favor strict separation between church and state but would allow all kinds of religious groups to compete for adherents. Finally, religious minimalists wish to maintain a separation of church and state and would restrict the free exercise of religious groups.

We can get an even clearer picture of this issue by moving beyond the scales that measure these attitudes and instead seeking to identify distinct sets of individuals based on their responses to each of the questions in the surveys. We have used cluster analysis to identify groups of individuals who share the same views on many of these items in both the Washington, D.C., and the Williamsburg Charter data. Because the Washington, D.C., survey contained a richer variety of free-exercise questions, we will rely on those data for the discussion below, but the same general result was evident in the Williamsburg data as well.

Cluster analysis allows the researcher to identify many small sets of individuals or fewer larger ones. There are general rules for selecting the best solution, which may have few or many clusters, but to do so it is necessary to estimate results with varying numbers of clusters. We conducted a series of analyses, identifying a range of numbers of clusters. We had posited four ideal positions and were pleasantly surprised to find that the best fit was a four-cluster solution that identified groups that matched each of our ideal types.

The four clusters were roughly similar in size although there were slightly more religious nonpreferentialists.[2] Nonpreferentialists were distinctive in their support for free-exercise rights for Christian and non-Christian groups—children who wish to wear religious headgear, Hare Krishnas soliciting at airports, conscientious objectors to war, children whose religious beliefs prohibit them from pledging the flag, Christian Scientists who wish to withhold medical treatment from their children, and Jews who wish to miss work on High Holidays.[3] They were also the most likely to agree to an abstract right to practice religion and to disagree that individuals should obey laws that restrict their religious freedoms. This group was also generally supportive of religious accommodation and was distinctively supportive of public displays of the menorah, funding for Buddhist chaplains, and allowing student religious organizations to use school property for their meetings. They were also the most strongly opposed to a high wall of separation between church and state. This group was composed primarily of well-educated, white Catholics and very liberal black pentecostals. Thus, the group of respondents who most clearly regarded religious accommodationism as a component of religious free exercise were not evangelical Protestants but rather those who have been the historical victims of discrimination. Recall that in chapter 3 our analyses of the Williamsburg data suggested that non-whites and Roman Catholics were the most likely to support "helping all religions equally" but were generally skeptical about support for a Judeo-Christian tradition. Moreover, the data presented in chapter 5 revealed that Catholics and pentecostals were most supportive of the free-exercise rights of religious minorities.[4]

The other three groups were almost identical in size. The Christian preferentialists were supportive of all accommodationist positions but were distinctively supportive of government help for religion, government protection of a Judeo-Christian heritage, prayer at high-school sporting events, a mandate to teach Judeo-Christian values and creationism in schools, a moment of silence in schools, funding for Christian chaplains, public displays of nativity scenes, and religious leaders picketing "pornographic" bookstores. They were opposed to the accommodation of non-Christian groups: Christian preferentialists were the least likely to support funding for Buddhist chaplains, and a narrow plurality opposed displays of the menorah. They were opposed to free-exercise rights for non-Christian groups and even for liberal Christians: They were distinctively opposed to allowing for conscientious objectors to war, allowing children to opt out of the pledge of allegiance, and allowing Native Americans to use peyote in their religious services, and they were most likely to indicate that individuals should obey laws that limit their religious freedom and to believe that immigrants should convert to Christianity. Christian preferentialists were primarily active members of orthodox Protestant churches, held orthodox religious identities, and were born again and believed that the Bible was literally true. They were older than the other three groups and less well educated. Again, it will be recalled that in chapter 3 evangelical Protestants were most supportive of preserving the nation's Judeo-Christian heritage. Thus, both the Williamsburg and Washington area data suggest that evangelical Protestants (the core constituency for groups such as the Moral Majority and the Christian Coalition) do not appear to regard the public accommodation of religious beliefs as an element of a generalized free exercise of religion. While activist leaders such as Falwell or Reed and scholars such as Carter might make the argument that the public accommodation of religious beliefs is simply a defensive reaction against social trends and government policies that have made religious free exercise more difficult, our data suggest that evangelical Christians are most likely to wish to create (or restore) a conservative Christian cultural hegemony.

Our focus-group data, as well as evidence from other sources, suggest that many accommodationist evangelical Christians are not generally supportive of the free-exercise rights of groups outside a presumed cultural consensus. As one woman noted, "I want prayer back in the schools, but there are so many religions now. . . . We pray to Jesus. Someone else prays to some other statue. I don't want my son praying to Buddha" (Dowd 1994). A recent *Newsweek* survey showed that many Christians "would not be upset if Congress passes a constitutional amendment permitting prayer in public schools that is offensive to non-Christians and non-believers" (Sedgwick 1994, 40). Many of our focus-group respondents expressed approval of concrete instances of accommodationism (school prayer, public religious displays) because they simply did not believe that such actions could be considered controversial.

Thus, our data suggest that many evangelical Christians have a communalist understanding of the nature of religious free exercise and may regard religious accommodationism as the prerogative of a presumed cultural majority. Indeed, it might be argued that the term "Moral Majority" is quite revealing in this context (see Jelen 1993a, 14).

The religious free-marketeers were also easily identifiable. They were distinctive in their opposition to government aid to religion, to government support for a Judeo-Christian heritage, and in their support for a high wall of separation between church and state. They were the least likely to favor public displays of the menorah and the nativity, were the least likely to favor funding for Christian chaplains, and opposed funding Buddhist chaplains as well. They were distinctive in their opposition to teaching creationism, a moment of silence, and prayers at high-school sporting events. They were also supportive of free-exercise rights of Christian and other groups and were especially distinctive in their support for Native Americans to use peyote in their religious services, in their opposition to requiring that immigrants convert to Christianity, and their opposition to laws banning cults from converting teenagers and banning Satan worship. They were also quite supportive of allowing fundamentalist preachers access to college campuses though not quite as supportive as the religious nonpreferentialists. This group of Washington area residents were especially well educated, disproportionately Jewish, and quite secular. They were distinctively low in frequency of church attendance, in doctrinal orthodoxy, and even in affiliation with a particular denomination.

Some may find the high level of support for free exercise by this largely secular group to be surprising. Although the high level of education of these citizens suggests support for civil liberties of unpopular groups, much of the elite discourse among cultural conservatives has suggested that secular, well-educated Americans are hostile to organized religion. However, we find that rather than being hostile to religion, this relatively secular group is quite supportive of free exercise in instances that do not seem to involve questions of religious establishment. This support for religious freedom extends to conservative Christian groups as well.

Finally, the group we labeled religious minimalists were also identified in the analysis. These citizens took separationist positions on most issues involving questions of religious establishment and were especially distinctive in their opposition to allowing student religious groups to use school property for their meetings. They were also opposed to free exercise by all kinds of groups, including fundamentalist ministers preaching on college campuses, Jews who wish to miss work on High Holidays, cults that seek to attract teenaged members, and Hare Krishnas soliciting at airports. Although this general pattern initially appeared to us to be a generalized pattern of opposition to all religion, in fact the individuals in this cluster ranked second in frequency of church attendance, in orthodox religious identities, in belief in biblical inerrancy, and in education. They were somewhat more likely than other groups to be found in Baptist and pentecostal churches. Although it is often argued that people who wish to minimize the public role of religion are hostile to religion, the religious profile of minimalists did not fit such a stereotype. Rather, the relatively high percentage of Baptists in this cluster leads us to believe that many minimalists are motivated by support for religious separatism, defined as a *theological* belief that good Christians should be separated from the sinfulness of the secular world (see Jelen 1987; Peshkin 1986). While we lack data in this study to test this supposition directly, we hypothesize that such people have a "sanctuary" approach to religion (see Roozen, McKinney, and Carroll 1984) and do not wish to see their beliefs and practices contaminated by involvement in public affairs. In other words, religion is an important, but very private, matter outside the realm of politics. Regardless of the validity of this hypothesis, however, our most important finding is that our data lead us to reject firmly the hypothesis that people who seek to minimize the public role of religion are either irreligious or antireligious and that those who are secular are hostile to religion.

Beyond the Culture War

Recent analyses have suggested that religious values and beliefs are assuming increasing importance in American politics. It has been suggested the axis of American political conflict is shifting from the economically based New Deal coalition to one based on cultural or moral values (see Hammond, Shilbey, and Solow 1994). In such a "culture war" (Hunter 1991), the most important political distinction is thought to be drawn between the "orthodox" and the "seculars" or between the religious and not so religious. Indeed, some analysts have argued that the *degree* of religiosity is becoming more politically important than the particular denomination or religious tradition to which an individual might belong (Kellstedt et al. 1994).

Whatever the validity of these broader claims, our data suggest that such a division is not useful in understanding public attitudes toward church–state relations. Indeed, the division between the religious and irreligious is misleading. Americans do differ with respect to religious belief and religious adherence but also disagree over the style and extent of engagement of religion in the public sphere. Our cluster analyses have shown that all of the cells of the four-fold typology described in chapter 1 are manifested in our empirical data. This correspondence between theory and evidence is quite gratifying and perhaps constitutes the best evidence that the public does have coherent attitudes on the relationship between God and Caesar.

Religiosity and religious orthodoxy are related to an accommodationist understanding of the establishment clause. Although this finding has exceptions, people who are highly religious are likely to see nothing wrong with certain policies in which government assists or promotes the public expression of religious belief. Indeed, our data suggest that a formidable coalition of white evangelicals, African Americans, and Roman Catholics might be quite favorably predisposed toward certain government supports for religious belief, as might be surprising numbers of more secular citizens.

However, our data suggest there is no consensus on the underlying rationale for the approval of such policies. As argued by Reed, Carter, and others, some respondents appear to regard a narrow interpretation of the establishment clause as an extension of the right of religious free exercise. However, it may be somewhat surprising that accommodationists who exhibit generalized support for free exercise generally are not the constituency of the Christian Right but are members of religious and racial minorities who have historically been the victims of discrimination.

Although it has been argued that doctrinally conservative Christians are the victims of discrimination (see especially Carter 1993) and have been denied some free-exercise rights by a separationist reading of the establishment clause, our data suggest that those evangelicals who support religious accommodation do not exhibit generalized support for the right of religious free exercise for those outside of the Judeo-Christian tradition. Rather, their understanding of the appropriate public role of religion appears to be communalist and, indeed, majoritarian. The pattern of responses of this group of evangelicals suggests that, within this cluster, a presumed Judeo-Christian or Christian majority has certain prerogatives that religious and cultural minorities must respect.

Further, our data suggest that irreligious or secular citizens are not necessarily hostile to public expressions of religion, provided such expressions do not receive government support. Our cluster of religious free-marketeers is easily the most secular of our four groups and is most clearly defined by its opposition to government accommodation of religion. However, this group also characteristically has a great deal of respect for the private practice of religion and appears to believe that government ought to protect such private religious prerogatives very carefully. Even highly irreligious people seem to regard religious belief as quite important and tend to believe that the enforcement of government policies should be tempered to respect religious free exercise. Conversely, we were quite surprised to find that the group apparently most hostile to government accommodation, or an expansive sense of free-exercise rights, was not particularly irreligious. Contrary to the expectations of the "culture wars" thesis, such respondents appeared rather religious and religiously orthodox. Again, we suspect that this group is motivated by a strong sense of the autonomy of the sacred rather than disapproval of religion generally.

What all of this appears to mean is that, at the level of public opinion, questions of religious establishment and free exercise are empirically, as well as conceptually, distinct. This distinction further suggests that there will be internal divisions within a coalition of the "religious." Doctrinally conservative Christians appear to hold highly majoritarian beliefs about the relationship between religion and politics or to regard the sacred and the secular as mutually incompatible spheres of human activity. As such, evangelicals are rather unlikely allies in political struggles for the free-exercise rights of religious minorities in an increasingly diverse religious mosaic.[5] Rather, Jose Casanova (1994) comes close to the mark when he characterizes evangelical Protestantism as the *de facto* civil religion of the United States. Similarly, religious minorities, be they Asian immigrants, Native Americans, or adherents of "cults" or "New Age" religions, seem unlikely to support the culturally hegemonic aspirations of some conservative Christians. A broad understanding of the free-exercise clause connotes an America characterized by a high degree of religious pluralism while the evangelical basis for religious accommodationism may be based on a belief in cultural consensus. Given such divisions in public opinion, we suspect that the *types* of religion practiced by Americans will continue to be as politically important as the *extent* of their religiosity.

Notes

1. The *Smith* decision upheld an Oregon law that legislated against the use of peyote and held that Native Americans whose religious rituals involved the use of the hallucinogenic drug were not exempt from the law.

2. We would remind readers at this point that our estimates of the relative size of the clusters may be affected by the fact that these data were gathered in the greater Washington, D.C., area and may not represent the American population as a whole.

3. It is important to remember that these individuals were disproportionately likely to take these positions but did not necessarily hold these positions in an

absolute sense. Thus most nonpreferentialists opposed allowing Christian Scientists to withhold medical treatment, but they were more likely than the other three groups to support this right.

4. Analysis of the four clusters reveals that African-American respondents were generally divided between the religious nonpreferentialist and Christian preferentialist clusters.

5. It is perhaps noteworthy that although some evangelical interest groups supported the Religious Freedom Restoration Act (a congressional response to the *Smith* decision), our data suggest that evangelical Christians at the mass level were relatively unlikely to support the legal use of drugs for religious purposes.

Appendix

Williamsburg Charter Survey
(Demographic and political items excluded)

(1) Generally speaking, how interested are you in current national politics? --very interested, somewhat interested, or not so interested?

(2) What pops into your mind when you hear the words "the First Amendment to the U.S. Constitution"? [Probe:] Anything else?

(3) How important is it to you that the next President be someone who has strong religious beliefs? Is it very important, somewhat important, or not important?

(4) If a Presidential candidate belongs to a political party you like and has many views you like, would you be willing to vote for such a person if the person is married and has been having other love affairs?

(5) If a Presidential candidate belongs to a political party you like and has many views you like, would you be willing to vote for such a person if the person has been a minister of a church?

(6) How about if the candidate is Catholic?

(7) How about if the candidate is a born-again Baptist?

(8) How about if the candidate is an atheist and does not believe in God?

(9) How about if the candidate is Jewish?

(10) How about if the candidate is a homosexual?

(11) How about if the candidate is Greek Orthodox?

(12) Which of these statements comes closest to your opinion? "The government should not provide any support to any religions." -- or -- "The government should support all religions equally."

(13) Do you think democracy in the United States works better if Americans are religious, or does it work worse if Americans are religious, or doesn't religion make any difference?

(14) [If "better" with religion, ask:]

Would you say religion is "absolutely required" for American democracy to work well -- or that it is "helpful but not required" for democracy?

(15)   In the United States Constitution, some freedoms are spelled out and some are not. Do you happen to recall if the freedom of religion is in the Constitution?

(16)   [If "yes," ask:]

Do you happen to recall if the freedom of religion is guaranteed by the First Amendment?

(17)   In the United States today, do you think there is any religious group or any other group that is a threat to democracy?

[Probe for specific groups, but do not read list]

[Atheists]
[Baptists]
[Born-Again Christians]

[Catholics]
[Communists]
[Cults & Sects]
["Fundamentalists"]

[Jews]
["Moonies"]
["Moral Majority/Falwell"]
[Mormons]
[Satan Worshipers]
[Secular Humanists]
[TV Preachers]

[Other:]

_____

[Don't Know]

(18)   **[If group named, ask:]**

Do you think some of their public activities should be restricted?

I'd like to read you some statements and I'm interested in whether you mostly agree or mostly disagree with each statement. By the way, if you don't have an opinion, please feel free to say so.

(19)   Here's the first statement:

"I would personally like to see organized religious groups stay out of politics." Would you say you "mostly agree" or "mostly disagree" with that statement?

(20)   "Religious groups should have a legal right to get involved in politics." Would you say you "mostly agree" or "mostly disagree"?

(21)   "It's good for Congress to start sessions with a public prayer."

(22)   "It's good for sporting events at public high schools to begin with a public prayer."

(23)   "There should be laws to prevent groups like Hare Krishna from asking people for money at airports."

(24)   "The Supreme Court is the best place to decide controversies about the separation of church and state."

(25)   "Churches should have to pay taxes on all their property."

(26)   "There should be laws against the practice of Satan worship."

(27)   "Followers of the Reverend Sun Myung Moon should not be allowed to print a daily newspaper in Washington, D.C."

(28)   "It's OK for a City Government to put up a manger scene on government property at Christmas."

(29)   "It's OK for a City Government to put up candles on government property for a Jewish religious celebration."

[Note: If respondent wants to change answer in the Christmas question, after being asked the Jewish candles question, please say "OK" and note the wish to change the answer here only:]

[Wants to change previous answer]

(30)   "It should be against the law for preachers to use television shows to raise money."

(31)   "It should be against the law for unusual religious cults to try to convert teen-agers."

(32)   "The influence of religion on American politics threatens to divide us as a country."

(33)   "There's less religious tolerance today than there was 20 or 30 years ago."

(34)   "It bothers me when TV and movies use the words 'Jesus Christ' to express anger or surprise."

(35)   "There is no place in America for the Moslem religion."

(36) "Churches should be denied their tax exemptions if they prevent women from becoming ministers or priests."

(37) "It's OK for the Right to Life movement to use religion in the debate about abortion."

(38) "It's OK for religious leaders to hide immigrants from Latin America when the U.S. government says those immigrants are illegal."

(39) "Most politicians today who talk about their own religious values are hypocrites."

(40) The government should require that Judeo-Christian values be emphasized in public schools.

(41) "People who hold strong religious beliefs tend to be intolerant of people who hold different beliefs."

(42) "The FBI should keep a close watch on new religious cults."

(43) "Public schools should allow student religious groups to hold voluntary meetings in school classrooms, when classes are not in session."

(44) "The group called the Moral Majority should stay out of politics."

(45) "The ACLU--the American Civil Liberties Union--files too many law suits regarding religion."

(46) "Public schools should set aside a moment of silence each day for students to pray if they want to."

(47) "It's OK for Jewish groups to give money to politicians who support Israel."

(48) "Reincarnation is something I personally believe."

(49) Do you think public schools should only teach the Bible's account of the creation of life on earth, or should they only teach evolution, or should they teach both?

(50) Many grade schools and high schools around the country are run by various churches and religious groups. Do you think the government should provide financial help to these schools?

(51) Do you think it's OK for the government to pay for chaplains for the military?

(52) [If "yes," ask:]

       Do you think it's OK for the government to pay for some Buddhist chaplains for the military?

[Note: If respondent wants to change answer in the first
chaplain question, after being asked the Buddhist chaplain
question, please say "OK" and note the wish to change the
answer here only:]

[Wants to change previous answer]

(53)   Are you familiar with the term "secular humanism"?

         [If "yes," ask:]

(54)   Do you think the public schools are teaching the values of
         "secular humanism"?

(55)   Do you think "secular humanism" has a good or bad impact on
         this country?

(56)   Do you think "secular humanism" should have the same rights
         and restrictions as a religion?

(57)   Do you think it is proper for religious leaders to publicly
         support political candidates who are running for office?

(58)   Do you think it is proper for religious leaders to try to
         influence U.S. policy toward South Africa?

(59)   Do you think it is proper for religious leaders to try to
         close pornographic book stores?

(60)   Which of these statements comes closest to your opinion?
         "The government should take special steps to protect the
         Judeo-Christian heritage." -- or -- "There should be a high
         wall of separation between church and state."

(61)   Do you think TV and newspapers are often unfair to religious
         groups?

         [If yes:] Which ones?
         [Probe:] Any others?   [Go to next page]

         [Neglect all religion]
         [Unfair to all religion]
         [Atheists]
         [Baptists]
         [Born-Again Christians]
         [Catholics]
         [Cults & Sects]
         ["Fundamentalists"]
         [Jews]
         ["Moonies"]
         ["Moral Majority/Falwell"]
         [Mormons]
         [Secular Humanists]
         [TV Preachers]
         [Other:]

(62)   Are there any religious groups in America that you think have <u>too much power and influence</u>?

> [Atheists]
> [Baptists]
> [Born-Again Christians]
> [Catholics]
>
> [Cults & Sects]
> ["Fundamentalists"]
> [Jews]
> ["Moonies"]
>
> ["Moral Majority/Falwell"]
> [Mormons]
> [Secular Humanists]
> [TV Preachers]
> [Other:]
> _____
> [Don't Know]

(63)   How important is religion in your daily life? Is it very important, somewhat important, or not at all important?

(64)   What is your religious preference or denomination, if any?

> PROTESTANT / CHRISTIAN
> **[If "Protestant" or "Christian" only, ask:]**
> Could you please tell me which denomination you think of yourself as closest to?
>
> **[If denomination is on this page ask:]**
> Have you ever had what you would call a "born again" religious experience?
>
> Do you believe the Bible is literally true, word for word?
>
> **[If "Catholic," ask:]**
> Do you think the Pope's teachings are infallible?
>
> **[If "Catholic," also ask:]**
> Have you had what you would call a "born again" religious experience?
>
> **[If "Jewish," ask:]**
> Is that Reformed, Conservative, or Orthodox?
>
> **[If "Jewish," also ask:]**
> Do you usually observe the rules of Kosher?

(65)   About how often do you attend religious services--about every week, once or twice a month, a few times a year, or never?

(Demographic and political variables excluded)

Please tell me whether you strongly agree, agree, disagree, strongly disagree, or neither agree nor disagree with each statement. If you have no opinion on a statement, please tell me.

    1.) Strongly agree
    2.) Agree
    3.) Neither agree nor disagree
    4.) Disagree
    5.) Strongly disagree
    9.) No opinion

1. People have the right to practice their religion as they see fit, even if their practices seem strange to most Americans.

2. The government should not provide help to religion.

3. Public school children should be permitted to wear religious headgear such as skullcaps or turbans to school if they want to.

4. In the interest of security, the FBI should infiltrate all Moslem groups in America.

5. Public schools should set aside a moment of silence each day for students to pray if they want to.

6. It should be against the law for unusual religious cults to try to convert teen-agers.

7. Public schools should allow student religious groups to hold voluntary meetings in school classrooms when classes are not in session.

8. It's OK for a city government to put up a manger scene on government property at Christmas.

9. It is important for people to obey the law, even if it means limiting their religious freedom.

10. In wartime, those whose religious beliefs forbid them from killing should be excused from military service.

11. It's good for sporting events at public high schools to begin with a public prayer.

12. It's OK for the government to pay for some Buddhist chaplains for the military.

13. If their religious beliefs forbid seeing doctors, Christian Scientists should be allowed to withhold medical treatment

from their children.

14. America is a Christian nation, and those who move here from other countries should be encouraged to convert to Christianity.

15. Jews should be allowed to stay home from work on the High Holy days, such as the Jewish New Year, even though these are workdays for most people.

16. The American Indians should be allowed to continue taking peyote, an illegal drug made from cactus plants, in their religious ceremonies.

17. It's OK for a city government to put up candles on government property for a Jewish religious celebration.

18. Public school children should be required to pledge allegiance to the American flag, even if this is against their religious beliefs.

19. We should maintain a high wall of separation between church and state.

20. The government should require that Judeo-Christian values be emphasized in public schools.

21. There should be laws against the practice of Satan worship.

22. Fundamentalist preachers should not be allowed to preach on college campuses in an attempt to convert young people.

23. The government should protect our Judeo-Christian heritage.

24. It's OK for the government to pay for Christian chaplains for the military.

25. It is OK for religious leaders to picket and boycott stores that sell books and magazines that these leaders believe are pornographic.

26. Public schools should teach creationism as an acceptable alternative to evolution.

27. There should be laws to prevent groups like the Hare Krishna from asking people for money in airports.

28. People have the right to practice their religion in the way they see fit, even if this involves sacrificing animals to their gods.

29. How frequently do you attend church services?

    1.   never
    2.   a few times a year
    3.   a few times a month

4.   almost every week
5.   every week

30. What is your religious preference or denomination, if any?
     (IF BAPTIST -- any particular Baptist denomination?)

31. Some Christians have had an experience which they call a born-
     again experience, and others have not. How about you? Have
     you had a born-again experience?

32. Which comes closest to your views of the Bible?

     1.   The Bible is the inspired word of God, and is literally
          true, word for word.
     2.   The Bible is the inspired word of God and has no errors,
          but some of it is meant to be taken figuratively.
     3.   The Bible is inspired by God, but contains human errors.
     4.   The Bible is not the word of God.

33. Do any of these terms describe your religious beliefs?

     a.   liberal Christian
     b.   fundamentalist Christian
     c.   evangelical Christian
     d.   charismatic or pentecostal Christian

34. Some Americans have had spiritual experiences such as speaking
     in tongues, healing by faith, or being slain in the Spirit.
     Other deeply religious Americans have not had that experience.
     How about you?

References

Asher, Herbert. 1992. *Presidential Election in American Politics: Candidates and Campaigns since 1952.* 5th ed. Pacific Grove, Calif.: Brooks-Cole.

Bardes, Barbara. 1992. "The Gender Gap in Support for the Gulf War." Presented at the Conference on the Consequences of the Gulf War, Brookings Institution, Washington, D.C.

Barry, Brian. 1990. "How Not to Defend Liberal Institutions." *British Journal of Political Science* 20: 1–14.

Beatty, Kathleen, and Oliver Walter. 1988. "Fundamentalists, Evangelicals, and Politics." *American Politics Quarterly* 16: 43–59.

Bendyna, Mary E., and Celinda C. Lake. 1994. "Gender and Voting in the 1992 Presidential Election." In *The Year of the Woman: Myths and Realities,* ed. E. Cook, S. Thomas, and C. Wilcox. Boulder, Colo.: Westview.

Benton, J. Edwin, and John L. Daly. 1991. "A Question-Order Effect in a Local Government Survey." *Public Opinion Quarterly* 55: 640–42.

Berelson, Bernard, Paul Lazarsfeld, and William McPhee. 1954. *Voting.* Chicago: University of Chicago Press.

Berger, Peter. 1967. *The Sacred Canopy: Elements of a Sociological Theory of Religion.* New York: Doubleday.

Biskupic, Joan. 1994. "Special School District Ruled Unconstitutional." *Washington Post* June 28: A1, A10.

Bork, Robert H. 1990. *The Tempting of America: The Political Seduction of the Law.* New York: Free Press.

Bradley, Gerard V. 1987. *Church–State Relationships in America.* Westport, Conn.: Greenwood.

Brady, Henry E., and Paul M. Sniderman. 1985. "Attitude Attribution: A Group Basis for Political Reasoning." *American Political Science Review* 79: 1061–78.

Brisbin, Richard A. 1992. "The Rehnquist Court and the Free Exercise of Religion." *Journal of Church and State* 34: 57–76.

Bruce, Steve. 1993. "Religion and Rational Choice: A Critique of Economic Explanations of Religious Behavior." *Sociology of Religion* 54: 193–205.

Carter, Stephen L. 1993. *The Culture of Disbelief: How American Law and Politics Trivialize Religious Devotion.* New York: Basic Books.

Casanova, Jose. 1994. *Public Religions in the Modern World.* Chicago: University of Chicago Press.

171

Chapman, Stephen. 1991. "Returning Religious Intolerance to Class." *Indianapolis Star* November 15: A6.

Conover, Pamela J. 1984. "The Influence of Group Identifications on Political Perceptions and Evaluations." *Journal of Politics* 46: 760–85.

———. 1988. "Feminists and the Gender Gap." *Journal of Politics* 50: 985–1010.

Conover, Pamela J., and Stanley Feldman. 1984. "How People Organize the Political World: A Schematic Model." *American Journal of Political Science* 28: 95–126.

Converse, Philip. 1964. "The Nature of Belief Systems in Mass Publics." In *Ideology and Discontent,* ed. D. Apter. New York: Wiley.

Cook, Elizabeth Adell. 1993. "The Generations of Feminism." In *Women in Politics: Outsiders or Insiders?* ed. L. Duke. Englewood Cliffs, N.J.: Prentice Hall.

Cook, Elizabeth Adell, Ted G. Jelen, and Clyde Wilcox. 1992. *Between Two Absolutes: Public Opinion and the Politics of Abortion.* Boulder, Colo.: Westview.

Cook, Elizabeth Adell, and Clyde Wilcox. 1991. "Feminism and the Gender Gap: A Second Look." *Journal of Politics* 53: 1111–22.

Cord, Robert L. 1982. *Separation of Church and State: Historical Fact and Current Fiction.* New York: Lambeth Press.

Curry, Thomas J. 1986. *The First Freedoms: Church and State in America to the Passage of the First Amendment.* New York: Oxford University Press.

Dahl, Robert A. 1982. *Dilemmas of Pluralist Democracy: Autonomy vs. Control.* New Haven, Conn.: Yale University Press.

David, Rene, and John E. Brierly. 1978. *Major Legal Systems of the World.* New York: Free Press.

Dowd, Maureen. 1994. "Americans Like G.O.P. Agenda, but Split on How to Reach Goals." *New York Times* December 15: A1, A14.

Elifson, Kirk, and C. Kirk Hadaway. 1985. "Prayer in Public Schools: When Church and State Collide." *Public Opinion Quarterly* 49: 317–29.

Erikson, Robert S., Norman R. Luttbeg, and Kent L. Tedin. 1991. *American Public Opinion.* New York: Macmillan.

Falwell, Jerry. 1980. *Listen, America!* Garden City, N.Y.: Doubleday.

Finke, Roger. 1990. "Religious Deregulation: Origins and Consequences." *Journal of Church and State* 32: 609–26.

Finke, Roger, and Rodney Stark. 1992. *The Churching of America, 1776–1990.* New Brunswick, N.J.: Rutgers University Press.

Fleet, Elizabeth, ed. 1946. "Madison's 'Detached Memoranda,' " *William and Mary Quarterly* 3: 535–62.

Friendly, Fred W., and Martha J.H. Elliot. 1984. *The Constitution: That Delicate Balance.* New York: Random House.

Germond, Jack W., and Jules Witcover. 1993. *Mad as Hell: Revolt at Ballot Box, 1992.* New York: Warner Books.

Gilbert, Christopher. 1993. *The Impact of Churches on Political Behavior.* Westport, Conn.: Greenwood.

Glendon, Mary Ann. 1991. *Rights Talk.* New York: Free Press.

Glock, Charles T., and Rodney Stark. 1966. *Christian Beliefs and Anti-Semitism.* Westport, Conn.: Greenwood.

Green, John C. 1993. "Pat Robertson and the Latest Crusade: Religious Resources and the 1988 Presidential Campaign." *Social Science Quarterly* 74: 157–68.

Greenawalt, Kent. 1988. *Religious Convictions and Political Choice.* New York: Oxford University Press.

Greenhouse, Linda. 1994. "High Court Bars School District Created to Benefit Hasidic Jews." *New York Times* June 28; A1, D21, D22.

Guth, James. 1984. "The Politics of Preachers: Southern Baptist Ministers and Christian Right Activism." In *New Christian Politics,* ed. D. Bromley and A. Shupe. Macon, Ga.: Mercer University Press.

———. 1989. "A New Turn for the Christian Right? Robertson's Support from the Southern Baptist Ministry." Presented at the annual meeting of the American Association for the Advancement of Science, San Francisco.

Hadden, Jeffrey K. 1969. *The Gathering Storm in the Churches.* Garden City, N.Y.: Doubleday.

Hamilton, Alexander, James Madison, and John Jay. 1937. (1791) *The Federalist.* New York: Modern Library.

Hammond, Phillip E., Mark A. Shibley, and Peter M. Solow. 1994. "Religion and Family Values in Presidential Voting." *Sociology of Religion* 55: 277–90.

Hart, Roderick. 1977. *The Political Pulpit.* West Lafayette, Ind.: Purdue University Press.

Hertzke, Allen D. 1993. *Echoes of Discontent: Jesse Jackson, Pat Robertson, and the Resurgence of Populism.* Washington, D.C.: CQ Press.

Himmelstein, Jerome. 1986. "The Social Basis of Anti-Feminism." *Journal for the Scientific Study of Religion* 25: 1–15.

Hirsley, Michael. 1993. "Prisons Fear Law to Restore Religious Rights." *Chicago Tribune* August 1: 1,4.

Hougland, James G., Jr. 1992. "The State and Observations of Religious Holiday Traditions: Attitudes toward Nativity Scenes on Government Property." *Sociological Analysis* 53: 299–308.

Hunter, James D. 1983. *American Evangelicalism: Conservative Religion and the Quandary of Modernity.* New Brunswick, N.J.: Rutgers University Press.

———. 1987. *Evangelicalism: The Coming Generation.* Chicago: University of Chicago Press.

———. 1990. "The Williamsburg Charter Survey: Methodology and Findings." *Journal of Law and Religion* 8: 257–71.

———. 1991. *Culture Wars: The Struggle to Define America.* New York: Basic Books.

———. 1994. *Before the Shooting Begins: Searching for Democracy in America's Culture War.* New York: Free Press.

Hurwitz, Jon, and Mark Peffley. 1987. "How Are Foreign Policy Attitudes Structured? A Hierarchical Model." *American Political Science Review* 81: 1099–120.

Iannaccone, Laurence. 1990. "Religious Practice: A Human Capital Approach." *Journal for the Scientific Study of Religion* 29: 297–314.

Jelen, Ted G. 1987. "The Effects of Religious Separatism on White Protestants in the 1984 Presidential Election." *Sociological Analysis* 48: 30–45.

———. 1989. "Biblical Literalism and Inerrancy: Does the Difference Make a Difference?" *Sociological Analysis* 49: 421–29.

―――. 1990. "Religious Belief and Attitude Constraint." *Journal for the Scientific Study of Religion* 29: 118–25.

―――. 1991a. *The Political Mobilization of Religious Beliefs.* New York: Praeger.

―――. 1991b. "Religion and Democratic Citizenship: A Review Essay." *Polity* 23: 471–81.

―――. 1993a. *The Political World of the Clergy.* New York: Praeger.

―――. 1993b. "The Political Consequences of Religious Group Attitudes." *Journal of Politics* 55: 178–90.

―――. 1994. "Religion and Foreign Policy Attitudes: Exploring the Effects of Denomination and Doctrine." *American Politics Quarterly* 22: 381–400.

Jelen, Ted G., and Clyde Wilcox. 1993. "Preaching to the Converted: The Causes and Consequences of Viewing Religious Television." In *Rediscovering the Religious Factor in American Politics,* ed. D. Leege and L. Kellstedt, Armonk, N.Y.: M.E. Sharpe. 255–69.

Kaukus, Dick. 1989. "Most Think Judge Erred in Crèche Case." *Lexington (Ky.) Herald-Leader* February 9: A1, A20.

Keilstedt, Lyman. 1989. "The Meaning and Measurement of Evangelicalism: Problems and Prospects." In *Religion and Political Behavior in the United States,* ed. T. Jelen. New York: Praeger.

Kellstedt, Lyman A., John C. Green, James L. Guth, and Corwin E. Smidt. 1994. "It's the Culture, Stupid: 1992 and Our Political Future." *First Things* 42 (April): 28–33.

Kilpatrick, James J. 1993. "One More Look at a Famous Wall." *Indianapolis Star* July 10: A8.

Kirk, Russell. 1986. "Introduction." In *The Assault on Religion,* ed. K. Russell. New York: University Press of America.

Kluger, Richard. 1977. *Simple Justice.* New York: Vintage Books.

Kosmin, Barry A., and Seymour P. Lachman. 1993. *One Nation under God: Religion in Contemporary American Society.* New York: Harmony Books.

Langenbach, Lisa. 1989. "Evangelical Elites and Political Activism: The Pat Robertson Presidential Campaign." Paper presented at the annual meeting of the Society for the Scientific Study of Religion, Salt Lake City, October.

Langenbach, Lisa, and John C. Green. 1992. "Hollow Core: Evangelical Clergy and the 1988 Robertson Presidential Campaign." *Polity* 25 147–58.

Leege, David C., and Lyman A. Kellstedt. 1993. "Religious Worldviews and Political Philosophies: Capturing Theory in the Grand Manner through Empirical Data." In *Rediscovering the Religious Factor in American Politics,* ed. D. Leege and L. Kellstedt, Armonk, N.Y.: M.E. Sharpe, 216–31.

Levy, Leonard W. 1986. *The Establishment Clause.* New York: Macmillan.

―――. 1988. *Original Intent and the Framers' Constitution.* New York: Macmillan.

Lijphart, Arend. 1975. *The Politics of Accommodation: Pluralism and Democracy in the Netherlands.* 2nd ed., revised. Berkeley: University of California Press.

Lindsay, Thomas. 1991. "James Madison on Religion and Politics: Rhetoric and Reality." *American Political Science Review* 85: 1231–337.

Lipset, Seymour Martin. 1960. *Political Man: The Social Basis of Politics.* New York: Doubleday.

Lipset, Seymour Martin, and Earl Raab. 1978. *The Politics of Unreason.* 2nd ed. Chicago: University of Chicago Press.

McClosky, Herbert, and Alida Brill. 1983. *Dimensions of Tolerance.* New York: Russell Sage.

McClosky, Herbert, and John Zaller. 1984. *The American Ethos: Public Attitudes toward Capitalism and Democracy.* Cambridge, Mass.: Harvard University Press.

McDowell, Gary L. 1993. "The Explosion and Erosion of Rights." In *The Bill of Rights in Modern America,* ed. D. Bodenhamer and J. Ely, Jr., 18–35. Bloomington, Ind.: Indiana University Press.

McFarland, Sam G. 1981. "Effects of Question Order and Survey Responses." *Public Opinion Quarterly* 45: 208–15.

McNamara, Patrick H. 1992. *Conscience First, Tradition Second: A Study of Young Catholics.* Albany, N.Y.: SUNY Press.

Malbin, Michael. 1978. *Religion and Politics: The Intentions of the Authors of the First Amendment.* Washington, D.C.: AEI Press.

Mannheim, Karl. 1972. "The Problem of Generations." In *The New Pilgrims,* ed. P. Altbach and R. Laufer. New York: David McKay.

Martin, Alfred R., and Ted G. Jelen. 1989. "Knowledge and Attitudes of Catholic College Students Regarding the Creation–Evolution Controversy." In *Religion and Political Behavior in the United States.* ed. T. Jelen, 83–92. New York: Praeger.

Miller, Arthur H., Patricia Gurin, Gerald Gurin, and Oksana Malanchuk. 1981. "Group Consciousness and Political Participation." *American Journal of Political Science* 25: 494–511.

Monsma, Stephen V. 1993a. "Justice Potter Stewart on Church and State." Paper presented at the annual meeting of the American Political Science Association, Washington, D.C., September.

———. 1993b. *Positive Neutrality: Letting Religious Freedom Ring.* Westport, Conn.: Praeger.

Morganthau, Tom. 1993. "America: Still a Melting Pot?" *Newsweek* August 9: 16–23.

Morken, Hubert. 1994. "Compromise: The Thinking Behind Colorado's Amendment #2 Strategy." Paper presented at the annual meeting of the American Political Science Association, New York, September.

Neuhaus, Richard John. 1984. *The Naked Public Square.* Grand Rapids, Mich.: Eerdmans.

———. 1992. "A New Order of Religious Freedom." *First Things* 20: 13–17.

Nunn, Clyde, Harry Crockett, Jr., and Allen Williams. 1978. *Tolerance for Nonconformity.* San Francisco: Jossey-Bass.

Ostling, Richard N. 1991. "What Does God Really Think about Sex?" *Time* June 24: 48–50.

Payne, Stanley. 1980. *The Art of Asking Questions.* Princeton, N.J.: Princeton University Press.

Perry, H.W. 1991. *Deciding to Decide: Agenda-Setting in the United States Supreme Court.* Cambridge, Mass.: Harvard University Press.

Peshkin, Alan. 1986. *God's Choice.* Chicago: University of Chicago Press.

Pfeffer, Leo. 1967. *Church, State, and Freedom.* Boston: Beacon Press.

————. 1979. "The Current State of Law in the United States and the Separationist Agenda." *The Annals* 446 (December): 1–9.

————. 1983. *Religious Freedom.* Lincolnwood, Ill.: National Textbook Company.

————. 1984. *Religion, State, and the Burger Court.* Buffalo, N.Y.: Prometheus Books.

Prothro, J., and C. Grigg. 1960. "Fundamental Principles of Democracy: Bases of Agreement and Disagreement." *Journal of Politics* 22: 276–94.

Quinley, Harold E. 1974. *The Prophetic Clergy: Social Activism among Protestant Ministers.* New York: Wiley.

Reed, Ralph. 1994. *Politically Incorrect: The Emerging Faith Factor in American Politics.* Dallas: Word.

Reichley, A. James. 1985. *Religion in American Public Life.* Washington, D.C.: Brookings.

Robbins, Thomas. 1993. "The Intensification of Church–State Conflict in the United States." *Social Compass* 40: 505–27.

Roelofs, H. Mark. 1992. "The Prophetic President: Charisma in the American Political Tradition." *Polity* 25: 1–20.

Roozen, David A., William McKinney, and Jackson W. Carroll. 1984. *Varieties of Religious Presence: Mission in Public Life.* New York: Pilgrim Press.

Rozell, Mark, and Clyde Wilcox, eds. Forthcoming 1996. *The Christian Right in the 1994 Elections.* New York. Rowman Littlefield.

Savage, David G. 1993. *Turning Right: The Making of the Rehnquist Supreme Court.* New York: Wiley.

Schuman, Howard, and Stanley Presser. 1981. *Question and Answers Attitude Surveys: Experiments in Question Form, Wording, and Context.* New York: Academic Press.

Schuman, Howard, Stanley Presser, and Jacob Ludwig. 1981. "Context Effects on Survey Responses to Questions about Abortion." *Public Opinion Quarterly* 45: 215–23.

Schumpeter, Joseph. 1950. *Capitalism, Socialism, and Democracy.* New York: Harper and Row.

Sedgwick, John. 1994. "The G.O.P.'s Three Amigos." *Newsweek* (January 9): 38–40.

Shapiro, R.Y., and H. Mahajan. 1986. "Gender Differences and Policy Preferences: A Summary of Trends from the 1950s to the 1980s." *Public Opinion Quarterly* 50: 42–61.

Sigelman, Lee. 1981. "Question Order Effects on Presidential Popularity." *Public Opinion Quarterly* 45: 119–207.

Smidt, Corwin. 1980. "Civil Religious Orientations among Elementary School Children." *Sociological Analysis* 41: 25–40.

————. 1982. "Civil Religious Orientations and Children's Perception of Political Authority." *Political Behavior* 4: 147–62.

————. 1988. "Evangelicals vs. Fundamentalists: An Analysis of the Political Characteristics and Importance of Two Major Religious Movements within American Politics." *Western Political Quarterly* 41: 601–20.

————. 1989. "'Praise the Lord' Politics: A Comparative Analysis of the Social Characteristics and Political Views of American Evangelical and Charismatic Christians." *Sociological Analysis* 50: 53–72.

Sniderman, Paul M., Richard A. Brody, and Philip E. Tetlock. 1991. *Reasoning and Choice: Explorations in Political Psychology.* New York: Cambridge University Press.

Sniderman, Paul M., and Philip E. Tetlock. 1986. "Interrelationship of Political Ideology and Public Opinion." In *Political Psychology: Contemporary Problems and Issues,* ed. M.E. Hermann, 62–96. San Francisco: Jossey-Bass.

Stark, Rodney, and James C. McCann. 1993. "Market Forces and Catholic Commitment: Exploring the New Paradigm." *Journal for the Scientific Study of Religion* 32: 111–24.

Stouffer, Samuel. 1955. *Communism, Conformity, and Civil Liberties.* New York: Doubleday.

Sullivan, John, James Pierson, and George Marcus. 1982. *Political Tolerance and American Democracy.* Chicago: University of Chicago Press.

Tajfel, Henri. 1970. "Experiments in Intergroup Discrimination." *Scientific American* 223: 96–103.

———. 1981. *Human Groups and Social Categories.* Cambridge: Cambridge University Press.

Tinder, Glenn. 1989. *The Political Meaning of Christianity.* Baton Rouge, La.: Louisiana State University Press.

Tocqueville, Alexis de. 1945. (*De la Démocratic en Amérique.* Paris: Charles Gosselin, 1835) *Democracy in America.* ed. P. Bradley. 2 vols. New York: Vintage Books.

Toolin, Cynthia. 1983. "American Civil Religion from 1789–1981: A Content Analysis of Presidential Inauguration Addresses." *Review of Religious Research* 25: 39–48.

Tribe, Laurence, and Michael C. Dorf. 1991. *On Reading the Constitution.* Cambridge, Mass.: Harvard University Press.

Urofsky, Melvin I. 1993. "Church and State: The Religion Clauses." In *The Bill of Rights in Modern America,* ed. D.J. Bodenhamer and J.W. Ely, Jr., 57–71. Bloomington, Ind.: Indiana University Press.

Wald, Kenneth. 1992. *Religion and Politics in the United States.* 2nd Edition. Washington, D.C.: CQ Press.

Wald, Kenneth, Dennis Owen, and Samuel Hill. 1988. "Churches as Political Communities." *American Political Science Review* 82: 531–49.

———. 1990. "Political Cohesion in Churches." *Journal of Politics* 52: 197–212.

Way, Frank, and Barbara Burt. 1983. "Religious Marginality and the Free Exercise Clause." *American Political Science Review* 77: 654–65.

Welch, Michael R., and David C. Leege. 1991. "Dual Reference Groups and Political Orientations: An Examination of Evangelically Oriented Catholics." *American Journal of Political Science* 35: 28–56.

Wilcox, Clyde. 1988. "Seeing the Connection: Religion and Politics in the Ohio Moral Majority." *Review of Religious Research* 30: 47–58.

———. 1989. "Feminism and Antifeminism among Evangelical Women." *Western Political Quarterly.* 42: 147–60.

———. 1991a. "Religion and Electoral Politics among American Blacks in 1988." In *The Bible and the Ballot Box,* ed. J.L. Guth and J.C. Green, 159–72. Boulder, Colo.: Westview.

———. 1991b. "Support for Gender Equality in West Europe: A Longitudinal Analysis." *European Journal for Political Research* 20: 127–47.

——. 1992. *God's Warriors: The Christian Right in 20th Century America.* Baltimore: Johns Hopkins University Press.

——. 1993. "The Dimensionality of Public Attitudes toward Church–State Establishment." *Journal for the Scientific Study of Religion* 32: 169–76.

Wilcox, Clyde, Dee Allsop, and Joseph Ferrara. 1993. "Group Differences in Early Support for the Gulf War: A Longitudinal Analysis." *American Politics Quarterly* 21: 343–59.

Wilcox, Clyde, and Elizabeth Adell Cook. 1989. "Evangelical Women and Feminism: Some Additional Evidence." *Women and Politics* 9: 27–56.

Wilcox, Clyde, and Ted G. Jelen. 1990. "Evangelicals and Political Tolerance." *American Politics Quarterly* 18: 25–46.

Wilcox, Clyde, Sharon Linzey, and Ted G. Jelen. 1991. "Reluctant Warriors: Pre-Millenialism and Politics in the Moral Majority." *Journal for the Scientific Study of Religion* 30: 245–58.

Wills, Garry. 1990. *Under God: Religion and American Politics.* New York: Simon and Schuster.

Wimberly, Ronald C. 1976. "Testing the Civil Religion Hypothesis." *Sociological Analysis* 37: 341–52.

Wood, James E., Jr. 1990. *The First Freedom: Religion and the Bill of Rights.* Waco, Texas: J.M. Dawson Institute of Church–State Studies, Baylor University.

Woodrum, Eric, and Thomas Hoban. 1992. "Support for Prayer in School and Creationism." *Sociological Analysis* 53: 309–21.

Zaller, John R. 1992. *The Nature and Origins of Mass Opinion.* New York: Cambridge University Press.

Cases Cited

Abingdon Township School District v. Schempp 374 U.S. 203 (1963)

Allegheny County v. ACLU 492 U.S. 573 (1989)

Board of Education of Kiryas Joel Village School District v. Grumet __ U.S. __ (1994)

Brown v. Board of Education of Topeka 347 U.S. 483 (1954)

Cantwell v. Connecticut 310 U.S. 296 (1940)

Chicago, Burlington, and Quincy Railroad Co. v. Chicago 166 U.S. 226 (1897)

Church of the Lukumi Babalu Aye v. City of Hialeah 509 U.S. __, 113 S.Ct. 2217 (1993)

Edward v. Aguillard 482 U.S. 578, 107 S.Ct. 2573 (1987)

Employment Division v. Smith 110 S.Ct. 1595 (1990)

Everson v. Board of Education 330 U.S. 1, 67 S.Ct. 504 (1947)

Gitlow v. New York 268 U.S. 652, 45 S.Ct. 625 (1925)

Goldman v. Weinberger 475 U.S. 503 (1986)

Heffron v. International Society for Krishna Consciousness 452 U.S. 640 (1981)

Lamb's Chapel v. Center Moriches Union Free School District 113 S.Ct. 2141 (1993)

Lee v. Weisman 112 S.Ct. 2649 (1992)

Lemon v. Kurtzman 403 U.S. 602, 91 S.Ct. 2105 (1971)

Mapp v. Ohio 367 U.S. 643, 81 S.Ct. 1684 (1961)

Michael H. v. Gerald D. 109 S.Ct. 2333 (1989)

Minersville School District v. Gobitis 310 U.S. 586 (1940)

Planned Parenthood of Southeastern Pennsylvania v. Casey 112 S.Ct. 2791 (1992)

Reynolds v. U.S. 98 U.S. 145 (1879)

Roe v. Wade 410 U.S. 113 (1973)

Sherbert v. Verner 374 U.S. 338, 83 S.Ct. 1790 (1963)

U.S. v. Lee 455 U.S. 252 (1982)

U.S. v. Seeger 380 U.S. 163, 85 S.Ct. 850, 13 L.Ed. 2d. 733 (1965)

Wallace v. Jaffree 472 U.S. 38, 105, 105 S.Ct. 2479 (1985)

Weeks v. U.S. 232 U.S. 383 (1914)

Welsh v. U.S. 398 U.S. 333, 90 S.Ct. 1792, 26 L.Ed. 2d. 308 (1970)

West Virginia State Board of Education v. Barnette 319 U.S. 624, 63 S.Ct. 1178 (1943)

Wisconsin v. Yoder 406 U.S. 208, 92 S.Ct. 1527 (1972)

Zobrest v. Catalina Foothills School District 113 S.Ct. 2462 (1993)

Index

About the Authors

Ted G. Jelen is Professor of Political Science at Illinois Benedictine College in Lisle, Illinois. Widely published on religion and politics, feminism, and the politics of abortion, he is currently at work on a study in normative political theory relating democratic citizenship to Christian discipleship.

Clyde Wilcox is Associate Professor of Government at Georgetown University. He is the author of *God's Warriors;* coauthor of *Serious Money: Individual Contributors in American Politics* and *Between Two Absolutes: Public Opinion and the Politics of Abortion;* and coeditor of *Risky Business: PAC Decisionmaking in Congressional Elections.*